PROLOGUE

An Existential Dialogue with a Mirror Reflection

What happens the day after you quit your job, tear everything down, and find yourself clueless about what comes next?

This question haunted me as I stared into the mirror, meeting the gaze of a stranger with weary eyes, deep lines of worry, and a look that seemed lost. I was 24 years old and had just done exactly that: quit my job as a speechwriter, walking away from the dream job I'd desired for years.

To this stranger, I posed a question: "What do you desire? What are you in pursuit of?"

Reflecting on my childhood dreams, I remembered yearning to be significant and effect change in the world. Despite achieving my goals, a profound sense of emptiness pervaded me. "I'm not sure what I want anymore," my True Self confessed, a hint of melancholy in its tone. My ambition to change the world felt futile, drained by my current state of disillusionment.

"Where has all your striving led you?" I continued to probe. Despite being on the path to what many would consider success, I felt sad, unmotivated, and alienated from myself. It became clear: the suit and tie, the adherence to societal expectations and career-ladder climbing, were obscuring my true identity rather than revealing it.

"It's just not worth it," I told my reflection. "Not worth your precious time on this earth."

"How do you feel? Have you done justice to your time on earth? Have you dedicated yourself to making meaningful change, exploring your creativity joyfully during your brief stint on this spinning blue dot? Have you truly valued your time?" I doubted it. This wasn't about guilt (well, maybe a little)—the guilt of knowing I had settled for a life that felt safe but uninspired, the guilt of wasted potential, of leaving my creative instincts untouched and dormant. It wasn't a crushing guilt, but a quiet, persistent whisper reminding me that I wasn't fully honoring the fleeting time I had.

"Do you owe anything to others? No—not to your boss, your parents, or anyone else. Actually, that's not entirely true. You owe it to them, but more important, to yourself, to realize your true potential and introduce your authentic self to the world."

That's when my True Self began to stir. "Lately, I've felt as though I'm losing parts of myself, and I hardly recognize who I am anymore. My vibrancy, my essence, it's fading. Why am I relinquishing my identity for 'achievement' and 'success' as dictated by societal norms? Why accept the hand dealt to me instead of charting my own course?"

For too long, I played a role, forgetting it was all a game. Now, torn apart, I realized I had lost sight of myself in pursuit of

THE TIME IS NOW

A GUIDE TO HONOR YOUR TIME ON EARTH

ALEX LEVY

Through Conversations
Press

CONTENTS

achievement. But to what end? "Yes, I suppose I have," my awakening True Self acknowledged.

What's the next step? Completely dismantling everything seems rash, yet the uncertainty of what follows terrifies me. How will I sustain myself? The fear of disappointment, anxiety, and reverting to old patterns looms large, as self-expression and exploration seem daunting in a world obsessed with ego.

"I fear breaking this cycle," I admitted. My True Self sighed, acknowledging past attempts to change direction, only to end up back where I started.

The stranger in the mirror countered, "It won't be easy. It might be the hardest challenge you'll face. But if not now, when? If you continue on this senseless path, you'll miss out on being truly present, forming meaningful connections, and discovering the essence of a fulfilling future that aligns with your genuine self."

"I know. But hey, the devil you know is better, right?" My True Self hesitated.

"Absolutely not. Life is about embracing the unknown, the unformed...the void," the stranger declared. "When you're in harmony with yourself, doubt has no place. Trust in your faith, your intuition, and your innate abilities. By embracing your true identity and allowing yourself to share it with the world, you'll escape the mental prison you've constructed. Make a bold declaration to yourself and to others: "I trust in myself.""

With that, my True Self exited the room, ready to embark on a journey to unlock his creative potential.

Suddenly, I viewed the world through new eyes—an empty canvas awaiting the vibrant strokes of my truest self.

INTRODUCTION

Hi, I'm Alex Levy, creator of the podcast Through Conversations. In 2023, my life hit a crossroads. After two years as a speechwriter for a prominent public figure, and a stint at a corporate job, I felt trapped, like my life was being dictated by someone else's vision. So, I quit—a decision that felt terrifying and liberating all at once.

Fast forward to today: I've interviewed over 100 of the world's most brilliant minds on my podcast, which at the time of writing has over 75,000 subscribers and 25 million views. I've explored my creative passions through writing this book, doing stand-up comedy, and diving into topics that ignite my curiosity. This journey hasn't been easy, but it's been deeply rewarding, transforming not just my career but my entire outlook on life.

This transformation forced me to take a hard look at the world of work, and the future of it—what it represents, how it shapes us, and what it takes away. I began asking questions: Why does work feel so draining instead of fulfilling? Why do we chase promotions and productivity metrics often at the cost of our creativity and well-being? Why are so many people longing for human connection in a modern reality of interconnectedness and collaboration? Why has the concept of work not evolved to include our current —and upcoming—technological innovations?

These reflections led me to realizations about the modern workplace, especially for younger generations like Generation Z and Millennials—though these insights resonate far beyond just us.

Generation Z, my generation, is the latest generation to be introduced to the modern workplace. After my "initiation" to it, my impression was:

(1) The office seems to have been built for everything except work. People within the office engage in office politics, gossiping, and distraction. The office is merely a social space, not a productive one.

(2) People who have worked for years within the modern workplace have lost themselves, their essence, while chasing digits, promotions, and the approval of others (often their bosses) and competing with their co-workers.

(3) In a world of loneliness, people are yearning for human connection with others and themselves—which has inevitably made the office the place for social life.

(4) Today's workplace has yet to make creativity its core engine. Instead, the office seems to have become the graveyard for daring, creative ideas—and people.

(5) The term "work" has turned over a new leaf, and we have not embraced it, to the point where many feel drained by their career rather than nurtured by it. Once viewed as a means of personal fulfillment and contribution, it has increasingly become a system of relentless productivity and performance metrics.

Instead of adapting to this shift with practices that nurture creativity and well-being, we've doubled down on treating workers as mere cogs in a machine. This misalignment has left many feeling drained, disconnected, and unfulfilled, as their careers no longer provide the sense of purpose they once promised.

To my surprise, experiencing the modern workplace led me to an existential crisis. What I thought was my dream job turned out to be the opposite. The predetermined path that I had followed because I thought it would bring me success and fulfillment didn't suit me.

I recognize that older generations have been able to thrive in the traditional workplace and build an entire life that is quite enviable, according to standard metrics, such as steady income and home ownership. Data from the U.S. Census Bureau indicates that in 1990, 56.5% of Baby Boomers owned homes, whereas in 2022 homeownership rates for Millennials sat at 51.5% in 2022.[1]

My grandpa always told me that his proudest, most enjoyable moments were when he worked at a car dealership. He built his most meaningful relationships there; he also felt that his company cared for him and trusted him.

My uncle built a decades-long career in which he ultimately became a top executive, and that gave him satisfaction and fulfillment.

It is safe to say that for older generations—mainly Baby Boomers, Gen Xs, and some Millennials—this type of life structure was, as famous comedian Larry David said, "pretty, pretty good." As a result, older generations came to view work as a means to an end with the primary purpose of earning a living to provide for themselves and their families. Their stable careers served as the foundation and springboard that would enable them to enjoy their time on earth. For many of them, work is a necessity, not a pleasure. Their ideal vision of work equals sacrifice, is hierarchical, and must be constrained to a 9-to-5 schedule, five days a week. According to this model, work primarily takes place in the office.

For Gen Z and Millenials, the story of work is unfolding to be dramatically different than the one older generations, including the men in my family, experienced.

While older generations benefited from economic stability and growth that facilitated a traditional life structure, Millennials and Gen Z face a more uncertain economic landscape, changing job markets, and different priorities—which have led to a dramatically different story of meaning, career, and purpose.

Gen Z views work as a crucial extension of who we are and want to become: work, while still a necessity, must also be a pleasure.

Gen Z is known for its intense creativity, entrepreneurialism, and keen desire to engage in positive social activism. We are the first generation born with technology as a core component of our lives —and we are extremely good at it. In addition, we are highly conscious of social issues and are not afraid to use our voices for change.

We believe we are built to collaborate; we set aside corporate hierarchical schemes and are extremely flexible with our work structure, given our creativity and adaptability.

We are built to create.

As Gen Z and Millennials take up an increasing portion of the world of work, their work and life ethos has become more mainstream. And it's attracting many people from older generations.

Deep within all of us, we know there is more to life than building a 40-year career that doesn't appeal to our truest selves. We know that the blessing of being able to say "I am alive" deserves proper honoring—one that must include exploring our creative potential.

Our current relationship with work reflects a deeper truth about ourselves: We use work as a distraction and as an escape from the *real* work we should be doing; we choose to drown ourselves in busyness, which often serves as the perfect excuse not to look at ourselves in the mirror. Busyness, in the context of work, might mean overscheduling meetings, working overtime, skipping family gatherings to attend conferences or catch up with work, and obsessively looking for any possible route toward a promotion or a pay raise.

But busyness is not isolated to the work sphere. Busyness is a state of mind that has a hold on most of our attention. It has effectively hijacked how we see, and honor, our time on earth.

We have created the perfect, most rational excuses to soullessly waste our lives: We are *busy* fighting wars for ideological or territorial reasons; we are *busy* arguing about politics with one another on social media; we are *busy* virtue signaling without being virtuous.

We are *busy* not living.

Truth is, it is easier to drown ourselves in busyness than to choose a life focused on creating ourselves. We'd rather ignore our true nature—our creative nature—than fully immerse ourselves in what truly fulfills our souls.

It is easier to be *busy* than to be *alive*.

In many cases, we spend nearly a third of our lives "busy at work" at the expense of family time, our creative passions, and inner exploration. Modern work—the shift from traditional manual labor to a structured 9-to-5 regime within the confines of modern cubicles, where white-collar jobs predominate and career progress is often measured by promotions and hierarchical success—has replaced these pillars of quality living, forcing them to devolve into one: our place of employment.

In that narrow, sometimes stuffy and emotionless environment, we seek our sense of belonging: a community of friends and a place to explore our creativity.

Unfortunately, it has become clear that work was never designed to accommodate these multifaceted aspects of our lives. We drive ourselves mad by accepting our careers as bland substitutes for sincere, creative living. The more time we spend at work, the more we're prevented from enjoying greater connectivity with the world; our co-workers will never replace true friendships and community. Worst of all, our creative nature fades away, slowly but surely, under a traditional 9-to-5 life regime.

The internal dynamics of an office are fascinatingly complex, too. Almost four generations collide with each other for eight hours per day, five days a week, with each generation having its own perspective on what "a life well-lived" truly means.

Luckily for me, my epiphany occurred in my early twenties (not in my fifties, as happens to countless people). I believe this life crisis is latent throughout one's professional career, but it explodes all at once when someone realizes that they've spent half their lives playing a fictitious game that was not their true calling.

My existential crisis made me acutely aware, for the first time, that I am not an infinite being, and I should not live like one by prolonging the discovery of my true calling to chase senseless objectives like careerism, praise, or even a paycheck.

The idea of exchanging my time for money no longer sat well with me.

The idea of denying my vitality and creativity over trying to prove myself to my bosses no longer sat well with me.

Perhaps most important, the idea of playing a role, wearing a mask, and living a fractured, façade-led life no longer sat well with me.

Granted, we must earn a living. But making a living should not mean strangling our creative passions in exchange for financial stability. Nor should making space for our creative passions mean sacrificing financial stability.

That is why I wrote this book.

All generations could benefit from hearing a younger side of the story. I seek to express a story that prioritizes well-being over accomplishment, one that reveals that accomplishment in itself is a direct consequence of our well-being. A guide that inspires us to embrace the sacred nature of our time on Earth, and that presents the uniqueness and necessity of honoring that time through the exploration—not repression—of our creative spirit, which is our true nature as a species.

When I discussed these ideas with older generations, they were received with open arms, and that inspired me to write a book that pays homage to all our lives—our relationship to the workplace, ourselves, each other, and our innately creative nature. Instead of feeling threatened by the prospect of such themes, older generations expressed eagerness to read more.

And so, here is my offering. *The Time Is Now* allows you to embark on a journey of the heart, a leap of faith that dares you to dream—not merely exist.

For too long, we have neglected our true nature: We are a creative force, not a workforce. We can solve our greatest challenges—as far as worldwide conflicts—solely through creative engagement. Unlike the office politics games we play, being creative *beings* sets us up for success on a planetary scale in multiple ways, the first one being that exploring our creativity is a positive-sum game that compounds over time and delivers aftershocks on a collective scale that uplifts, inspires, and fills us with a joy for life.

I hope to inspire you, whether you are nineteen or far past sixty-nine, to tap into the unspoken, unrealized aspects of yourself.

To embrace your creative nature.

To unleash the creative god that lives inside you—one the whole world desperately needs.

This book is built upon the ideas of the world's most creative individuals. It leverages brilliant ideas taken from interviews on my podcast, Through Conversations—where I have interviewed some of the world's most brilliant minds—pop-culture, movies, other books, and thought-leaders—and chimpanzees—and seeks to grapple with big, existential questions while making you laugh every now and then. It is also shaped by in-depth research and my own personal journey.

I spent over 2 years researching the intricate dynamics of the modern workplace, reviewing hundreds of sources on topics ranging from technological innovation to personal growth, and speaking with an array of individuals–from all backgrounds–who have grappled with the very questions this book seeks to address.

We'll explore the challenges that come with taking leaps of faith—how to identify and navigate through them. We'll explore the future of work that will be heavily impacted by technological innovation, such as artificial intelligence (AI), and some ways we can walk the talk of building a career based on our lives rather than our lives based on our careers.

This journey is divided into three parts: Part one is all about real-ization–this section is about awakening; It's the first step–under-standing what's fundamentally wrong with the path we're taking. Realization is the "aha" moment where we examine the societal scripts we've been handed and begin to question their relevance in our lives. Here, we dive deep into self-awareness, unpacking who we are, what motivates us, and how these influences have shaped our decisions. It's about shining a light on our blueprint—our internal wiring—and recognizing both its potential and limi-tations.

Part two covers integration: Integration is about acceptance and transformation. This is where we confront and embrace our shadow—the parts of ourselves we've ignored or repressed. By understanding our darker sides, motivations, and fears, we learn to integrate this knowledge into our lives without being controlled by it. It's about cutting the umbilical cord to what no longer serves us and transforming our newfound awareness into tools for personal growth. This stage is where the internal work begins, preparing us to act authentically and with integrity.

Part three is all about action. Awareness and acceptance mean nothing without action. This part is where we take everything we've uncovered and integrated, and put it into practice. Action is about aligning our lives with our creative potential and values; It's where we begin crafting a life that honors our time on Earth—one decision, one leap, one moment at a time.

This book isn't a step-by-step prescription or a rigid guide on how to live your life. It doesn't claim to have all the answers because, frankly, everyone's journey is different. The paths we walk are shaped by our unique experiences, dreams, and challenges. Instead, *The Time Is Now* is an invitation—a call to reflect, explore, and awaken to the possibilities that exist beyond the predetermined scripts handed to us.

I didn't want to write a "how-to" book because life doesn't come with instructions, and no one can tell you what your path should look like. What I can do is share stories, insights, and ideas to help you question the status quo and inspire you to take the first step toward living a life aligned with your true creative potential.

To further support your journey, each chapter concludes with reflective questions or key takeaways designed to prompt deeper introspection. These moments are not meant to direct you but to empower you, helping you uncover your truths and chart your own path.

I want to offer a caveat: some ideas in this book may feel repetitive at times, but that is intentional. To truly grasp where we are, where we want to go, and what it takes to unleash our creative potential, we must remind ourselves of the challenges we face, the opportunities ahead, and the reasons driving us forward. Repetition—when purposeful—is essential for fully digesting, internalizing, and acting on transformative ideas.

The Time Is Now is a call to action for *all* of us to turn the page on lives based on despair, disappointments, regrets, and procrastination and begin a new chapter of excitement, optimism, truth, courage, integrity, and loyalty to our souls.

But especially, a chapter built upon our creative nature.

Writing this book genuinely replenished my life's energy, and it is my sincere wish that these words transfer you that same energy—and that they help you awaken to the true wealth you already own–one that makes you unlimited with creative power.

I wish this book opens you to the realization of how precious your time on Earth is, and you Honor Your Time On Earth the only way it can truly be honored:

Your own way.

PART I

REALIZATION

INSTANTS

If I could live my life again,

In the next I'll try to make more mistakes,

I won't try to be so perfect,

I'll be more relaxed,

I'll be fuller than I am now,

In fact, I'll take fewer things seriously,

I'll be less hygienic,

I'll take more risks,

I'll take more trips,

I'll watch more sunsets,

I'll climb more mountains,

I'll swim more rivers,

I'll go to more places I've never been,

I'll eat more ice cream and less lima beans,

I'll have more real problems and less imaginary ones,

I was one of those people who lived a prudent and prolific life

Each minute of his life,

Of course, I had moments of joy,

But if I could go back, I'll try to have only good moments,

If you don't know, that's what life is made of.

Don't lose the now!

I was one of those who never go anywhere

Without a thermometer,

Without a hot-water bottle,

And without an umbrella and without a parachute,

If I could live again, I would travel light,

If I could live again, I'd try to work on bare feet

From the beginning of spring till the end of autumn,

I'll ride more carts,

I'll watch more sunrises and play with more children,

If I had the life to live, but now I am eighty-five,

and I know that I am dying ...

— A POEM BY JORGE LUIS BORGES

1

THE HARDEST BATTLE YOU WILL EVER FACE

To be nobody but yourself in a world which is doing its best day and night to make you like everybody else means to fight the hardest battle which any human being can fight and never stop fighting.

— *E.E. CUMMINGS*

As we transition from our teenage years, we embark on our journey into adulthood. Others expect us to begin a life based on a linear path carved out by our industrial-age ancestors: attend college, get married, have a decent-paying job, have kids, retire, and eventually...die.

At face value, this path seems enticing for teens, as they are eager to board the collective train of modern life and join the crowd. Most of our peers take this path, and as a society, we seem to put a premium on it.

Fast forward seven years later, when we turn twenty-five—another milestone birthday—and an unexpected internal clock starts ticking more intensely until we feel the pulse of time passing sensibly. More recently, for many—including myself—this is the first moment we awaken to our own mortality. Eighty-six percent of Millennials report having experienced a quarter-life crisis[1], the first moment in our lives when we realize we are not eternal beings and our time on Earth is fragile.

A life crisis could be described as a challenge to our assumptions about how life should unfold. We start asking ourselves:

"What have I done my entire life?"

"Why did I spend so much time building someone else's dreams instead of figuring out my own?"

"Where did all my creativity, my sense of agency, go?"

"Why did I not stand up for what I believe in?"

Some of us decide to change course based on what we learn during this challenging time, but many accept these feelings as a symptom requiring alleviation. So, instead of sitting with our emotions and exploring their root causes, we reach for pain killers —quick-fix remedies that temporarily numb the discomfort. These "pain killers" might take the form of distractions like binge-watching TV shows, retail therapy, excessive social media scrolling, or even pursuing a new career milestone solely for the sense of fleeting accomplishment it brings. Like an existential Tylenol or Advil, they provide relief but fail to address the deeper, unresolved issues at the heart of our unrest.

For a select few, a lightbulb moment illuminates their existence. This epiphany stems from a unique blend of factors: a passionate drive to dive into their craft, a profound understanding of time's true value, and a sharp realization of how society has squandered their time by compelling them to engage in meaningless pursuits of status and prestige.

Carl Jung, one of the most influential psychoanalysts in history and a figure we'll quote a few times throughout this book, brilliantly summarized this epiphany: These individuals realized that,

> "the shoe that fits one person pinches another; there is no recipe for living that suits all cases."

For some, it is up until we have a nervous breakdown that it dawns upon us that we realize the fragility and preciousness of our life. That we decide to "grab the bull by the horns," as my late grandpa used to say, and get on with building a life we are proud of.

My own understanding of such a crisis was first shaped as I witnessed my dad's midlife crisis.

From a young age, he was captivated by the world of computing, immersing himself in the intricacies of the Atari Model 1600, Intellivision, and Atari 3000. His childhood was filled with breaking down and understanding these machines, a passion that continued into his college years, when he created his own games featuring spaceships and snakes. Despite his deep-rooted interest in computing, a conversation with a close friend steered him toward a career in business.

He told my father something that made total rational sense: "You already know your computers, so it makes more sense to study business now and then pursue a master's in programming later." This argument convinced him to switch his major and pivot his entire life vision. He eventually became a businessman who owned a string of restaurant franchises—which was far removed from his passion for technology.

While my dad is extremely grateful for the success and fulfillment his franchises brought him, selling them at the age of forty was a pivotal decision driven by practicality and a desire for change. While it made sense as a smart business move at the time, it also left him confronting a deeper question: What's next? He found himself grappling with a midlife crisis, reflecting on how to channel his extensive knowledge of business and entrepreneurship, while also wondering what might have been if he had pursued his early passion for computing—a field that had always sparked his imagination. Today, he takes pride in the choices he made, particularly those that allowed him to spend invaluable time with his sons during their formative years and foster genuine friendships with the people he worked with.

He credits his midlife crisis as a pivotal moment in his life. From then on, he has immersed himself in community volunteering, coaching, and taking long walks. His priority is now his family, and he spends as much time as possible with us.

Any form of life crisis can be seen as a direct threat that needs to be overcome by any means necessary, as we perceive these challenges as a risk for our path toward success, and quite frankly, a threat to our false notion of sanity. "How can I keep making money, being productive if my heart aches?" "How can I finally get the promotion I desperately deserve if my heart constantly tells me that what I'm doing is not worth the effort?"

The very few people brave enough to tap into such feelings of existential dread receive an immeasurable reward after the storm passes: a true, integrated, self-respecting, self-deserving, self-loving map for the rest of their lives.

Some of the most "successful" people, defined by such common metrics as money, fame, wealth, and power, describe having a make-or-break moment when they decided to go all-in to explore their passion. And the paradox is so interesting: the more they fell in love with their craft, the more external success landed in the palm of their hands—it wasn't the main objective but instead a natural consequence of embracing their true nature:

Tim Ferriss, an American entrepreneur, investor, author, podcaster, and lifestyle guru, used to work as a salesman for a tech company. While the position earned him a six-figure salary, his job made him work exhaustively long hours with high-stress levels due to the constant pressure of meeting sales quotas. After some time, Tim became anxious, chronically stressed, and eventually fell into a depression.

When he wrote his bestseller, *The 4-Hour Work Week*, Tim shared how disillusionment ignited his desire to do a hard pivot in his life, take some time for himself—travel, and allow new possibilities to emerge within him.

During his sabbatical, Tim began to think about entrepreneurship, lifestyle design, and productivity. In hindsight, his decision may have looked easy, but taking a sabbatical can be quite hard and nonsensical when we have a high-paying, highly prestigious job. Still, Tim could not shake that feeling of uneasiness. Selfishly speaking, I'm glad he acted upon it as I have immensely benefited from his courage to break free from his conventional path. I hope to meet him one day and discuss some of these big, existential ideas.

Tim's decision to follow his heart massively paid off. Of course, it took him many years, but he has written several books, including *The 4-Hour Work Week*, which sold over 1.3 million copies and spent four years on the New York Times Best Seller list. Other books include *The 4-Hour Body*, and *Tools of Titans*, also bestsellers. Tim also became an angel investor in some of the world's most important companies, including Twitter and Shopify. He continued following his curiosity and started *The Tim Ferriss Show*, where he interviews outstanding people across multiple fields, including giants I genuinely admire, like Naval Ravikant, LeBron James, and Brené Brown. His show has been downloaded over five hundred million times.

Tim has been called one of the most innovative businessmen in the world. Today, he spends his time focusing on his creative interests and philanthropy. Thankfully, he continues to share his insights with the world, although it could be said he's already won the game of life through conventional metrics.

Julia Child (1912-2004) was an American chef, author, and television personality best known for bringing French cuisine to American home cooks. Before she was known for those accomplishments, Julia had a rewarding career in advertising and media. She worked for several media outlets, including the Office of Strategic Services, where she helped create various films related to World War II. She was married to Paul Child, who worked for the U.S. Information Service before he moved to France.

In her book, *My Life in France*, she wrote about feeling unfulfilled in her previous careers, making her more open to exploring new creative interests. Not knowing what to do with her free time, Julia enrolled in a cooking class, stumbling upon a surprising passion for cooking. She began to cook on her own, and in 1961, she published *Mastering the Art of French Cooking*, which became a bestseller and launched her career as a cookbook author and TV personality. Julia went on to host several cooking television shows, including *The French Chef*, which ran for over a decade.

Her contributions to the culinary world were widely recognized during her lifetime. She received numerous awards and honors, including the Legion of Honor from the French government, the Presidential Medal of Freedom from President Clinton, and induction into the Culinary Institute of America's Hall of Fame.

Her serendipitously discovered passion also influenced a new generation of cooks, including my best friend, who is now the head chef of a high-end restaurant.

Child's warmth, humor, and passion for cooking have inspired a new generation of home cooks and professional chefs who explore their creativity through the culinary arts.

Jay Shetty began his career in corporate marketing. As a young rising professional, Jay believed he was on the right track toward success, financial freedom, and recognition. Over time, however, these feelings dissipated, and a sense of disillusionment and deviation from his true purpose began to take center stage. Jay described feeling lost and unfulfilled, struggling with anxiety and depression, and turning to alcohol and partying as coping mechanisms.[2] He also felt disconnected from his cultural and spiritual roots, having grown up in a British-Indian family but feeling dissociated from his true heritage. Slowly, he began to adopt mindfulness practices and connected with his spiritual side.[3]

One day, Jay left everything behind—his prestigious job, salary, and bubble—and took a leap of faith by traveling to India, where he immersed himself in the world of spirituality, yoga, and inner self-discovery through his heritage. He spent three years traveling and studying to become a monk. Then, after some time immersing himself in timeless Buddhist wisdom, he rose like a phoenix from the ashes and found a new purpose: sharing his insights about self-discovery, finding one's purpose, and aligning one's life with one's values to ultimately inspire others to take their journey of self-exploration. Jay began sharing his lessons on social media, amassing thirty million followers on several platforms. He then wrote the New York Times bestseller *Think Like a Monk* and started his own podcast. Today, Jay acknowledges his deep sense of fulfillment and gives credit to his internal journey and the external success he now enjoys.

These three stories remind us that our true, sincere impact on other lives only comes from following our hearts and exploring new possibilities, allowing serendipity to guide us on the journey to our desired destination, where we witness our true colors emerge. When we remove the masks that enable role-playing and instead immerse ourselves in our true, sincere, authentic humanity, we push the boundaries of all our perceived limitations.

Tim, Jay, and Julia shed light on the possibility of allowing life to guide us—not in a clichéd sense, but in a real one. Their lack of fulfillment ignited their desire to explore their humanity, and I bet they didn't know how rewarding that decision would be for their time on Earth. If we were to ask them, "Would you give away all your external success and take a leap of faith just to feel a renewed sense of purpose in your life?" I bet they would say, "Yes!" without hesitation. External success was never their initial intention after quitting their jobs or moving to a new country. Instead, they wanted to explore their intuition, and in doing so, life itself rewarded them with unimaginable payoffs.

The Price of Progress

You might be thinking, "Hey, good for Tim, Jay, and Julia, but I can't just quit my job to find my passion." And trust me, I understand why. I'm no economist, but I do know the cost of living has increased. It seems that the conventional definition of the American Dream has never been as difficult to obtain as it is today. And let us remember how previous generations were able to achieve the American Dream in the first place—through hard work and long hours. Their blood, sweat, and tears enabled them to buy property, save for retirement, get married, buy a car, and afford a quality lifestyle—including decent, healthy meals, traveling, and access to quality education. During the 1960s, the average yearly family income was estimated at $5,600, and the median home price was $11,900. So, buying a home cost 2.1 times the average salary.[4] In 2022, the average family income was $70,784, and the median home price ballooned to $440,300. This meant that owning a home in 2022 rose to more than seven times the average salary.[5] Just like that, one fundamental piece of the American Dream became seemingly impossible to obtain in today's economy.

Now, let's examine another pillar of the American Dream: is it true that hard work pays off?

The average age of our grandparents, the Baby Boomers, was 33 years old during their peak years of productivity in the workforce.[6] Unlike Gen X, Millennials, and Gen Z, their hard work actually went into their pockets as productivity grew, and compensation was proportionate to the work produced. Productivity grew 118.4 percent from 1948 through 1979, and compensation increased by 107.5 percent during the same span, less than an 11 percent separation between work and pay.[7]

But, a switch flipped during the late 1970s.

A series of policies were implemented that changed the playing field to favor the top workers (CEOs from companies and other corporate executives) and shareholders. Federal minimum wages leveled off, tax rates for the top earners were lowered, and deregulation of many industries, including the trucking and airline industries, proliferated.

From 1979 through 2020, hourly pay increased 17.3 percent, while productivity rose 64.6 percent. In other words, productivity was 3.7 times the amount of pay. In a perfect world, wages should equal productivity, right? That is, the output should equal the input, or even surpass it.[8]

Where did all the excess potential earnings derived from productivity go? They had to go somewhere, right? Well, they swooped into the pockets of shareholders and corporate executives.

In a very real sense, the top 1 percent is reaping most of the rewards from the bottom 99 percent.

So, the notion of "hard work pays off" has also vanished. Productivity no longer equals higher pay. Another pillar of the American Dream, vanished.

What about saving for retirement? One of the coveted dreams for our grandparents was to become millionaires because it guaranteed a path to prosperity in the long term and, if they played their cards right, it could lead to generational prosperity. In 1979, $1 million had the purchasing power of over $4 million today. Therefore, to enjoy the same quality of life in 2023, we would need to earn approximately $4 million. This inflation means that being a "millionaire" today doesn't carry the same financial security as it did in the past. Currently, over 58% of Americans live paycheck to paycheck, highlighting the widening gap between income and cost of living.[9]

While education is one great means of upward mobility, earning a degree has never been as expensive as it is today. The average amount of student loan debt per borrower in the United States stands at $37,338. Over the past years, this figure has been consistently rising and has now reached its highest point ever. For individuals with a bachelor's degree, the average student loan debt is $32,731, whereas those with a master's degree carry an average student loan debt of $72,492. And it takes an average of over twenty years to repay that debt in full.[10]

The combination of these economic factors plays a major role in how younger generations view their relationship to their work and their life. What is the point of committing to a company when we know that excess productivity will not go into our pockets, but to a handful of people who don't even work within the company, but own a piece of it? Why commit to work for more than eight years—the average work tenure for Baby Boomers—when we know that our pension programs aren't as robust as they were for them, and our hard work does not equal good pay?

You might believe I dislike capitalism and that I think it should be changed into a different system. That is not the case. I am not against the notion that hard work, consistency, and effort can create wealth for anyone. It is by far the system that levels the playing field more than other alternatives in terms of making prosperity generally attainable.

However, we have been conditioned to believe we are productive assets rather than creative beings, and we could put some blame on capitalism for this, as it incentivizes economic growth over everything—prioritizing tangible, measurable objectives above all else.

We tend to be prioritized as employees, viewed as human capital— Human Resources—rather than creative forces of nature. For many, this is a perfect way of living, as it allows for some financial cushion and stability. Nonetheless, for people who have a burning desire to create, build and explore, it could mean doom. Stability and working to "make a living" rather than *feeling alive* are, for most of us, a death sentence.

I have worked within the corporate world and have always felt something was off, both with myself and the system in which I worked. I felt like a mesh inside a big machine and my efforts would just feed this machine, leaving me with a lifeless feeling.

We have torn our world apart, living off its beauty by dwelling in an economy of extraction rather than integration. *Integration* here means aligning ourselves with the natural flow of life, creating rather than depleting. Our natural resources are disappearing just as fast as our sense of self and creativity. But we must remember the Cree Indians' message:

> "Only when the last tree is cut down, the last fish caught, and the last river poisoned will we realize we cannot eat money."

We have to be careful with what game we choose to play, as it eventually finds its way to play us. Working just for a salary—which we have seen does not honor our hard work anymore—didn't work for me due to the transactional nature of that engagement. I felt that I would give up my time and earn money every two weeks, but I couldn't give it up while I waited eagerly for my paycheck. As Nassim Taleb, author of *Black Swan* asserts,

> "The three most harmful addictions are heroin, carbohydrates, and a monthly salary."[11]

On the flip side, capitalism does reward the best creation out there. If we tap into the power of our minds, explore what makes us feel we are living an authentic life and throw ourselves wholeheartedly into our craft, the remaining missing pieces, the monetary rewards, and the outpour of success will find their way to us and be perceived as something secondary to our path. We will collect these missing pieces, acknowledge and gladly accept them as the symbolic outgrowths of following our hearts.

These additional elements, whether they come in the form of relationships, material possessions, or career opportunities, will fulfill us when we recognize their inherent authenticity, and we freely declare, 'I choose freedom; I did what was right according to the dictates of my mind and heart.'

Rather than seeing our time on Earth as transactional, we can leverage the current systems to our advantage. Instead of fighting the current, we can immerse ourselves in the waters and create a current of our own, and our own definition of currency. How we do this is discussed in Part 3: Action, where we explore actionable steps to reclaim our time, redefine success, and align our lives with our true passions.

The biggest challenge—the hardest battle we will ever face—is meaningfully shaping that current and choosing to create our own lane. The games we play are almost always predetermined; the careers society asks us to choose are already set with their own terms and conditions and if you play those games, there will be rewards—but they will always come with a cost.

Remember: The games you play end up playing you.

If we choose to follow a predetermined path without being authentic, we risk losing key pieces of ourselves, including core values, talents, and perhaps even dreams. The most dangerous thing to lose is probably ourselves to an idea we don't even believe in, all because we unconsciously accepted that the reward was something we wanted without asking ourselves if it actually was our end goal. That's why most people choose to follow a pre-existing path—because few have built a strong foundation of self-reliance and self-awareness to envision what a meaningful life could look like otherwise. And without knowing what they want their life to be, they can become trapped by a work culture that prioritizes productivity over creativity.

The Alchemist's Secret: A Lesson in Living Your Dreams

> ... whoever you are, or whatever it is that you do, when you really want something, it's because that desire originated in the soul of the universe.
>
> — *PAULO COELHO*

Existential, creative crises are nothing new. Many authors have written about it in different ways, such as Paulo Coelho in his masterpiece, *The Alchemist*—one of my favorite books of all time.

The story follows a young shepherd, Santiago, who embarks on a journey to find his treasure and fulfill his personal legend—his larger purpose. For Santiago, his personal legend embodies his journey of inner growth and the fulfillment of his destiny, which is unveiled to him through a dream about finding a treasure. Along the way, he encounters various characters and experiences that teach him valuable lessons about the pursuit of one's dreams.

On his journey, Santiago encounters a crystal merchant, an old man whose own personal legend involves making a pilgrimage to Mecca. But like most of us, he never had the courage to search for it. Instead, the merchant decided to pause his vision of going to Mecca, allowing his fears and insecurities to overtake him; he opted to set up a crystal shop and settle for a comfortable life. The shop offered him stability and a good income, although it never gave him the real comfort he seeks, as his inner song still was living inside of him yearning to be let out. The crystal merchant regretted never starting his journey to Mecca, and this regret ate him alive throughout his whole life, soon forgetting about his personal legend.

At one point in the story, Santiago also loses sight of his personal legend while working in the crystal shop and becomes caught up in the immediate concerns and distractions of his job and daily routine. After encountering various obstacles and setbacks, he finds himself in a state of disillusionment and uncertainty, *living a life of quiet desperation.* He questions whether he should continue pursuing his dreams or settle for a stable but unfulfilling life.

However, this forgetting phase becomes an intricate part of Santiago's journey and represents a common struggle faced by those trying to discover ourselves and our personal legends: We momentarily lose sight of our purpose or become distracted by external circumstances. All too often, just like the crystal merchant, many of us ultimately become entangled by happenstance, lose sight of our genuine purpose, and cease the journey, never fulfilling our intended pursuit. Like the crystal merchant, people often passively let life happen to them instead of proactively making life happen for themselves.

As for Santiago, he remains true to himself, regains his focus, and recommits to his journey, ultimately finding the true treasure he has been seeking. He encounters it in his dreams at the very place where his journey began: an abandoned church in Andalusia, Spain.

More often than not, what we search for is right in front of us. In fact, it's *within* us. Although Santiago's travels and encounters throughout the story are necessary for his personal growth and an understanding of his own abilities and desires, the fact that he found the treasure right where his journey began reveals a powerful message: The true treasure was never a material possession, but the fulfillment of his personal legend and the discovery of his authentic self.

The internal journey is essential for unlocking our creative potential. It reveals our personal legends and exposes the truths about our current lifestyle—socially enforced behaviors that prioritize material productivity over creativity, prey on our fears and greed, and tempt us to abandon our dreams. Then, with seemingly nowhere to turn, we conform to external expectations and relinquish our unique gifts and abilities. As a result, we become fear-driven and comfort-seeking, giving into others' expectations and settling—just like the crystal merchant.

As Santiago shows us, our greatest treasure and source of fulfillment is to be found within our hearts, our intuition, and owning a sense of agency in our lives. All of us would do well to embody Santiago and heed the warning signs of a life ruled by fear, as the crystal merchant's experience exemplifies. Our personal legend exists within us—not just 'out there' in external space and time.

Modern Life: Productivity over Creativity

Remember that wherever your heart is, there you will find your treasure.

— *PAULO COELHO*

Let's get this out of the way: There is no such thing as a "dream job."

When I was working at my "dream job," a lack of internal fulfillment persisted daily, regardless of my accomplishments or how much I improved my productivity. Even though I had achieved all I ever wanted before my twenty-fifth birthday—attained "success" by any conventional definition—and my forward trajectory was enviably promising, I had never felt so empty and hopeless. These feelings crept up within me and wouldn't budge. Although people may have perceived me as "successful" on the outside, I felt like a failure inside.

I believe Tim Feriss, Julia Child, and Jay Shetty wished they had established a connection with their jobs when they first embarked on their conventional life paths as marketers and sales managers, just as I did. For some reason, they didn't. Their careers, like mine, were noteworthy and prestigious by society's standards, with high earning potential and universal recognition. I had high hopes that my dream job would make me feel alive and fulfilled. Despite my hard work, it left me feeling empty and without purpose.

The more I tried to rationalize my feelings, the more they kept growing larger and larger. The painful part of my story is that I realize millions of us live with these feelings every day. Moreover, society reinforces the idea that as we mature and become independent, we must view and accept these feelings and emotions as normal.

Many of my close relatives used to tell me, with the best of intentions, that everyone experiences these feelings, and eventually, as we keep climbing the ladder of life, they just fade into the background, essentially becoming a natural part of who we are. So, I followed the program, believing that my life's work was to blend with everybody else; I would not take my eye off the ball in reaching for my dream, willingly sacrificing every other aspect of my life.

In my approach to relationships and to friendships—my absence from family gatherings, evading my passions, and failure to invest my time in self-fulfilling pursuits, I manifested my belief in so-called conventional wisdom. My internal mantra was, "The more I sacrifice to be successful, the more success I will find."

Success was never for me, but for everyone else. I worked myself into a state of anxiety, depression, and isolation just because I wanted to reach a mythical top. I was sacrificing myself for an ideal that wasn't providing fulfillment. I felt as if I were losing crucial aspects of myself while climbing the proverbial ladder of success, and I stopped recognizing who I was and wanted to be. Paradoxically, my ideal vision was crushing my ideal self.

In modernity, most of us behave like the crystal merchant. With the concept of retirement hanging over our heads, we live a life in a state of deferred happiness. Our reasoning is not faulty at all: Before pursuing a craft or getting to know ourselves through our creative passions, we engage in some form of productivity throughout time, save for the rainy days and when we become silver-haired and amass enough money, we retire and embark on the self-introspective journey to discover our true essence. But that misguided life plan is like planting seeds in winter and expecting a rose garden.

We behave this way because of the laws of repetition—not because of the laws of nature. In the famous "Skinner Experiment,"where a rat was placed in a cage with a lever, and each time it would pull the lever, it would receive a food pellet. The rat began to associate the act with receiving a reward, making it obsessively repeat that behavior.[12]

Similarly, we have built our own cage through the way we live. But just like in Skinner's experiment, the reward rarely manifests when we *think* it should—regardless of how hard we pull the lever.

We behave this way because our system is driven by productivity, not by meaning or creativity. Yet, it is as clear as the blue sky that we ache for deep, rooted, creative purposes in life. Most of us don't realize how we spend our time on Earth; we get caught up in pursuing external markers of success that bring us worldly riches, but deplete us of our life force.

In reality, true wealth only arrives when our work emerges from a place of energy, when it has as its source our *Élan Vital*—our life force, one that makes us evolve as creative individuals.

The only way to achieve that goal is if we engage in activities that energize, not drain us.

We seem to perceive feelings of hopelessness and emptiness as immutable laws of nature—the inevitable consequences of living in the twenty-first century. In my own life, I have acknowledged these feelings as loyal companions throughout my early career.

Let's consider it on a macro scale. If today's collective successes, such as GDP growth, higher quality standards, and greater access to resources, have been meaningful, why do so many of us feel profoundly empty and experience a looming sense of despair in the world?

Could it be the case that our definition of success (that is, the notion that success through quantifiable metrics such as economic growth and wage increases that translate into gainful employment with a high upside and financial stability) is eating us alive?

Could it be that the definition of success we nurture is entirely flawed? Could it be that our erroneous definition is tied up with the complete unawareness that we are billionaires already as the wealth we amass derives from our *time on Earth, not from any digits on our bank account*?

Could it be that the very definition of success, as "conventional wisdom" defines it, is a systemic failure, and I am not the only one experiencing such hardship?

Such introspection during my brief time on this planet thus far has led me to the following convictions: I refuse to go to my grave with my song still inside me. What's more, I refuse to neglect going deeply within myself, and realizing (*or at least giving myself time to explore*) what my song truly may be. I refuse to accept that the song within me could go unnoticed for a lifetime; I refuse to accept that, just as me, billions of others have a unique song within them that could go unnoticed for their entire lifetime.

By accepting this as normal, we do a disservice to our time on Earth. We must redefine our definition of success—from pursuing success defined by external validation, to understanding the terms and conditions of achieving true greatness. We often see the upside of our visions but neglect the costs. We seek to gain more, attain more, amass more—the senseless pursuit of more, more, more. Sadly, the principles of Via Negativa, an idea explored in part three of this book, seem to be lost on us. Fortunately, we are rational beings, capable of expanding our minds and changing our behavioral patterns. I refuse to believe otherwise.

If we don't adjust our path, we risk losing our creative spark.

We have to face the music: Most jobs are not built for creativity, they are built for productivity. We are not being nurtured to be creative forces of nature. Instead, we are carefully engineered to be productive, artificial, and replaceable assets.

These circumstances draw a stark comparison to the Greek myth of King Sisyphus who was condemned to endlessly roll a boulder up a hill, only for it to roll back down each time he neared the summit. This myth illustrates the futility of repetitive, unending tasks, mirroring the often fruitless endeavors we encounter in our own lives and work.

We are creative by nature but are rapidly killing our most innate and pure talent.

We fast-forward through life, believing that the switch from creativity to productivity is not hurting our sense of self—both on a micro and macro scale—until we can't even recognize ourselves. We spend our adult lives chasing a treasure with fake gold, and when we get there, we realize how much we sacrificed for something that doesn't fulfill us.

But are we doomed to repeat Sisyphus' story for all eternity? Of course not!

We can break the cycle by learning to listen to our inner song—a tune that, once rediscovered, can guide us back to the creative, fulfilling life we are meant to live.

A Life of Quiet Desperation, or Intense Creative Enjoyment?

> Most people die at 25 and aren't buried until they're 75
>
> — *BENJAMIN FRANKLIN*

A "life of quiet desperation," is what sums up a life without creative exploration. Philosopher Henry David Thoreau (1817-1862), said that most men live an outwardly successful life but are filled with inner emptiness. In Thoreau's words,

> "the mass of men live lives of quiet desperation and go to the grave with the song still in them."

I believe that living without exploring one's inner song has killed more people than any other virus or war in the history of humankind.

This is true to the modern workplace. We may have a good-paying job, may own a nice home with friends and family surrounding us. But we can still experience a sense of emptiness and dissatisfaction—feelings that never leave us alone. Most of our jobs often are packed with meaningless, repetitive work; our capitalistic, bureaucratic system thrives upon it. But endless tasks within a cubicle may bring our creative spirits to their end.

These feelings, Thoreau would likely agree, are associated with living a life of quiet desperation, the calls of life from our inner song desperately pleading to be heard. Surprisingly, as many of us grow up, we assume we don't have an inner song worth exploring, or that our creative interests need to take second place to "serious pursuits." We drown ourselves in an ocean of compromises— necessary paychecks, meaningless tasks, and false praise, and we swim inside role-playing games few of us truly enjoy. Navigating this ocean, however stimulating it may be, is nonetheless artificial —and our heart knows it. But we dive so deeply within it that we keep lowering the frequency of our song until one day, it's totally muted.

On a macro scale, we can make the case that living a life of quiet desperation has created its own ripple effects, including car rage, atomized, lonely living; our obsession with material possessions (namely, money, prestige, and power), and chronic stress.

This too has permeated critical areas like public service, where many of our public officials are often viewed not as beacons of hope and integrity, but rather as corrupt, power-hungry, and self-interested.

Living an artificial life can make us feel like we are not living our true potential or that we are not making a positive difference in the world. And while not entirely quantifiable, I believe our modern problems stem from the style of life we have; from the disconnection we have between our lives and careers.

The realest danger of the modern workplace is that it makes us ignore our creative passions and mute our inner songs for an entire life—a life of quiet desperation.

But, as long as we have our song within us, there is still hope.

We must open our eyes to the truth about our time on Earth and nurture the idea that by exploring our creative passions, we honor it by turning up the volume on our inner songs. At the same time, we contribute to society in the most meaningful way. When we put ourselves first, we begin to put others first. To do that, however, we must first cherish every moment of our time on Earth, realizing that life is finite.

Pause and Ponder: Chapter One

• How do I personally define success? Does my current career path align with this definition?

• Where did I adopt my definition of success, and does it motivate or haunt me? How might I change it to better inspire and uplift my spirit?

• What activities or hobbies bring me joy, even on weekends? Could I incorporate more of these into my life?

• What inner song does my soul sing, and how can I tune into it more often?

• If I could craft my personal legend, like Santiago's journey, what story would I write for myself?

• How do I feel about the concept of retirement? Have I postponed any creative pursuits for that time, and how might I start engaging in them now?

2

OUR TIME WILL TIME US

The trouble is you think you have time.

— *BUDDHA*

In the back of our minds, we all entertain the thought that our time on Earth is finite. We recognize that we are mortal beings and will eventually cease to exist. We act based on this idea; some run from this realization, others embrace it, many do both. Some people avoid acknowledging it altogether by drowning themselves in stimuli-driven activities, such as sex and chasing positions of power, and indulging in instant gratification activities, like social media, or by engaging in excessive shopping and binge-watching television. Other people tend to embrace this idea and fully immerse themselves in their humanity, exploring what makes them tick and why they are here on Earth in the first place. Our desire to always *feel something* is directly related to our understanding that we will die.

I believe I fall in-between these two categories, as most people do. I've always known that my time on Earth is limited, but it really began to sink in when I left home to chase my dreams, and the thought became more present.

That sudden realization came to me in the middle of the night when I woke up from a nightmare. I asked myself, *If I had only a year to live, would I be doing what I am doing with my life?* The immediate answer, consciously and while dreaming, was a straight "no." My awakening to my own mortality hit me like a train. The way I saw my life changed forever. I started reflecting upon all my desires, goals, thoughts, and aspirations and examining how they were emerging within me.

This has been the most challenging thing I have ever experienced, as I began to closely question my ambitions: *Why do I feel the need to achieve anything in life? Why did I ever accept my goals as a uniquely natural part of who I am?*

I then realized that most of the aspirations I wanted to achieve were superfluous, tied up to an artificially driven desire to feel recognized, praised, and even respected—to make a name for myself and rise through the ranks of meaningless games we play. Most importantly, all these feelings were anchored to trying to hold on for dear life, as I thought they would make me live forever.

The truth is that most of the ambitions we have are nothing but pure air. They are as untouchable as the clouds above us. In the grand scheme of life, it doesn't matter if we have an amazing job title or if we embark on a great career trajectory. Think about it for a second: we are here on Earth for a mere seventy-five to one hundred years[1], which may seem like a long time, but in terms of cosmic time, it's nothing.

In an episode of my podcast, *Through Conversations*, I had the chance to explore the cost of relentless work with Kyle Kowalski, the founder of Sloww.co, a platform dedicated to promoting a more deliberate and thoughtful way of living.[2] Kyle shared his journey from a high-flying marketing professional to reaching a pivotal moment of existential questioning. For years, he thrived in a demanding career, but it was a relentless six-month period of sixty- to eighty-hour weeks that pushed him to his limits.

Each night, after long hours at work and only after his family had gone to sleep, Kyle would find himself working even more, often questioning the meaning of his efforts as he lay awake at 2 or 3 a.m. He described this intense period as one that forced him to confront the stark reality of his life's purpose. Ironically, while he was tasked with rejuvenating a century-old brand facing its own identity crisis, he was simultaneously grappling with his own. This irony did not escape him as he questioned whether his life's purpose was really about pushing consumerism—products to people they don't actually need—or if there was more he was meant to live for. This profound disconnect between his professional achievements and his personal fulfillment led Kyle to deeply question not just his career path, but his very reason for being.

For Kyle, up until his thirties, life was a project that had to be finished, and each promotion or bump in his paycheck was an indicator that his project was progressing. But therein lies the risk of treating life as a project that needs to be finished: The present moment is never treated as it should be, as a present. By constantly focusing on future goals and achievements, we fail to truly value the here and now, missing out on the joys and opportunities that each present moment offers. As a result, life becomes devoid of purpose and meaning, turning into a series of ironies and frustrations, where the genuine fulfillment we seek always seems just out of reach.

Kieran Setiya, a professor of philosophy at MIT, also shared insights on my podcast that profoundly shaped my understanding of life's purpose.[3] He explained that while projects like getting a promotion or publishing a book are important, they come with a paradox. We often focus so intently on future goals that our present becomes a landscape of continual dissatisfaction. Once a goal is achieved, it quickly becomes part of our past, leaving us without that moment of satisfaction we anticipated.

More critically, Setiya pointed out that if our sense of meaning is tied solely to reaching these endpoints, our efforts might paradoxically erase the very sources of meaning in our lives. This continual striving towards goals can feel like we're extinguishing the elements that give our life purpose. This realization struck a chord with me, reflecting on my own life filled with project-driven pursuits, and helped me understand the underlying causes of my existential crisis.

What Kyle, Kieran, and I have observed—and what many can likely relate to—is the pervasive societal belief that the present moment serves merely as a stepping stone towards achieving our future-oriented goals. This outlook reduces our current experiences to mere means to an end, overshadowing the intrinsic value of living in the now.

We don't realize until it's too late that we never actually asked ourselves the questions that truly matter in life, such as the one Kyle asked himself: Am I really on this planet for such a short time, only to sell people more stuff they don't really need?

Acknowledging the sense of despair that emerges from realizing how much time has been wasted on senseless chases, helps the truth begin to surface: *Why give my life away today for a superficial tomorrow? Why climb an invisible ladder of success? Why blindly follow the recipe everyone has for life, even though it is making me miserable, instead of figuring out my own?*

The great thing about our heart is that it never leaves us. When Kyle, Kieran, and myself experienced our existential crisis, a burning feeling remained that there actually is something 'out there' that connects to who we truly are that would allow us to thrive.

But our ways of living don't incentivize pursuing that "something." We witness a reversal of that inner calling based on greed and the acquisition mentality already discussed. "Hey, you'll likely fail, so it would be better for you to get a good-paying job and save a ton of money so later on you have the chance to do whatever you want."

In other words, we sacrifice passion, heart for money to then *hopefully* be able to sacrifice money for passion and heart.

We accepted such an act of surrender as a normal part of life, but the numbers behind this narrative reveal that the formula advocating for relinquishing our creativity for money may be failing us. Millions of people feel disconnected from life, community, and work, so they spend eight to ten hours daily in a place they hate.[4] Most of us maintain a façade of normality that society expects us to embrace.

Personally, I find that insane.

This "autopilot-dance-mode" leaves us feeling like puppets or extras in someone else's film—as if we are being *puppeted* into becoming a character, told what to do and say, and we often feel numb.

Every creative person has likely heard the mantra that life is better if we don't make anyone feel mad, stay in our lanes, and keep following protocols until we can remove all chains once we are in a position of authority. But that almost never happens—the chains just get a stronger grip on us.

Truth is, we have been transformed from a creative force into a productive asset, chasing false gods such as promotions, prestige, and power.

The real challenge for a true creative individual lies in acknowledging the golden chains that bind us and why we hold on to them so tightly.

Are our dreams really ours? Are our ambitions truly ours? Are we living life to its fullest, or just going through the motions on autopilot?

To help us resolve these questions, we will explore the journey of a famous leprechaun who crossed a rainbow in hopes of finding the treasure of his lifetime—only to find something much more surprising and enriching than any amount of gold.

The Myth of the Pot of Gold: The Lessons of the Leprechaun's Journey

> Value your time. It is all you have. It's more important than your money. It's more important than your friends. It is more important than anything. Your time is all you have. Do not waste your time.
>
> — *NAVAL RAVIKANT*

It's 3:00 a.m., and the line between my dream and real life is blurry: the clock is not ticking, yet feels as if it never stopped; the sheets feel light but hold me tightly. A sudden appetite for the Cereal Lucky Charms emerges while I battle a deep existential anxiety. The can't-avoid questions finally wake me up:

"What have I done during my entire life?"

"Where did all my creativity go?"

"If I had only a year to live, would I be doing what I am doing with my life?"

But the deepest question emerged: "I haven't eaten Lucky Charms in years...Why can't I stop thinking about them all of the sudden? Do I even *have* cereal?"

The immediate answer, consciously and while dreaming, was a straight "no." I did not buy Lucky Charms, and I would not continue doing what I was doing if I knew I had just one year to live.

My awakening to my own mortality—and the scarcity of Lucky Charms—hit me like a train conducted by a marshmallow-crazed leprechaun. The way I saw my life changed forever.

I believed I was meant to work for forty years at a job, saving for retirement, before I could finally pursue the creative passions I had sidelined while grinding away.

Just like a leprechaun who tirelessly chases the elusive pot of gold at the end of the rainbow, I believed that following the prescribed 'path to success' was my ticket to the American Dream. I thought the treasure awaited across the rainbow, attainable through hard work and perseverance.

When I think about my experience, and sudden need to eat Lucky Charms, I remember a specific scene from the movie *Click*.

Michael Newman (Adam Sandler) finds himself in the 'Beyond Storage Room' at Bed Bath and Beyond, where Morty (Christopher Walken) offers him a universal remote control that lets him fast-forward through life's "nonsense." Desperate for control, Michael uses the remote to skip moments with his family, intimacy with his wife, and time with his parents—all in pursuit of a promotion at work.

Morty warns Michael about chasing illusions, likening him to the leprechaun from "Lucky Charms," who braves challenges to find treasure at the end of the rainbow, only to discover it's just corn-flakes. Similarly, Michael realizes too late that what he was chasing —a better future—was already within reach: a loving family and meaningful moments he overlooked in his quest.

Many of us embrace Michael's reasoning: Once I get to be a partner at my firm, I'll finally be able to spend meaningful time with my family; I'll be able to have sufficient money to spend on them, take them on family trips, buy them whatever they want— the latest-model bicycles, new pets, etc.—and I'll be able to finish the life projects we worked on together, including a tree house.

I shared this mindset for a long time, too. I thought the faster I climbed the ladder, the freer I would be afterward, but that is absolutely *not* the case—quite the contrary: The more I saw myself becoming immersed within any mission not aligned with who I am, the less I saw myself enjoying more freedom, exploring my humanity—and ultimately honoring my time on Earth.

Talk about a profound message that has always been in front of us!

We tend to see that treasure as our ultimate means of fulfillment, but we never stop to recognize that we may have everything we need—and want—at this moment right in front of us.

On second thought, we acknowledge that truth, but our reasoning leads us to buy into the toxic notion that we will finally become whole when we cross the rainbow and grab the treasure.

The movie *Click* shows us how toxic the idea of achievement can become. We become blind to important parts of our lives that really matter and have a bigger place in our hearts than we thought: our family, our hobbies, our community, our passions.

This carrot-on-the-stick chase is nonsense. It is a root cause of many social problems faced today, from depression to anger, isolation to desperation. If we all were to tap into the power of our time on Earth and unleash our creative power, we would have the opportunity to thrive, and no longer postpone our enjoyment.

After reflecting on my dissatisfaction, I've reached a critical insight: "If I'm not content with my current situation, why do I believe that merely pursuing a distant 'treasure' will bring me happiness?"

In other words, as Naval Ravikant, a famous angel investor and entrepreneur, said,

> "If you are not happy with a cup of coffee right now, what makes you think you'll be fulfilled once you get a yacht?"[5]

Some people live under the false pretense that our loved ones will always be around. I'm realizing with ever-increasing intensity this is not true. Our passions, deep loves, relationships, and ties to our communities begin to fade away as we prioritize other aspects of life, leading us to fast forward through the things that really matter to us.

In our subconscious, we find ourselves grappling with two distinct roles. On one hand, we are the successful employee who diligently follows the rules and *robotically* climbs the corporate ladder. On the other hand, deep within, we yearn to embark on an internal journey to discover our real treasure—ourselves and our true passions.

Do you really believe that after putting on a mask for decades, you will finally be able to make a dent in the universe once you have enough money? There is no one alive that can win that battle. Think about it: If you play a role for forty years, you become that role, and the role becomes you. By the time you enter the final years of your career, you have become immersed in autopilot mode, living to work.

Society often normalizes sacrificing our creative spirits for up to forty years, just to pay bills and live a life devoid of creativity and personal fulfillment.

This modern chase for stability, wealth, and prestige has conquered our creative spirits.

The reality is that this system has a life of its own, and it has become a powerful driver of human behavior. When we spend an entire lifetime building an undesired career, we risk becoming our jobs. Once we do quit, we find ourselves not knowing how to live. In fact, there is a strong relationship between retiring and dying within a few years after retirement. In one study, it was discovered that individuals who retired at age sixty-five from some of the world's largest companies, including Boeing, AT&T, and Lockheed Martin, passed away, on average, less than two years after retiring. In other words, late retirees within these companies only enjoyed less than two years of freedom, powered by their pensions they so desperately were looking forward to enjoying. In contrast, those who retired by age fifty lived to be an average of eighty-six years old.[6]

This startling finding points to a profound, harsh truth: People who work too hard and are late retirees in a job they are not aligned with—and have probably endured more stress than they could handle—develop several chronic health problems.

When many people think about retiring, they feel that once they stop working and enjoy life, life will continue way into their golden years. Our bodies, minds, souls, and ways of living have become completely ingrained in our jobs, and have taken such an expensive toll that when we rip off the band-aid, we can't adapt to our new reality—a reality of freedom.

Although some studies have argued that working past sixty-five might be better for our health, the undeniable truth is that, as time passes, we become our jobs, and our jobs become us.[7] Nicole Maestas, an associate professor of health care policy at Harvard Medical School, believes that this mixed bag of results can be interpreted as a signal rather than noise: Maestas asserts that we must be smart about what we're doing:

> "Don't stay in a job you hate. Try to find something that's meaningful and gives you purpose. If you're happy at work, that's one sign that work may be good for your health."[8]

I completely subscribe to Maestas' philosophy: Work according to your desired goals and within your own boundaries. Numbers reveal, however, that most people feel unhappy at work and experience stress on a regular basis. One Gallup poll showed that stress and anxiety among workers are at an 'all-time high.'[9]

According to the combined information in those studies, most people are not doing the work they love and find themselves at a heightened risk of postponing true creative enjoyment for *decades*. When these people retire, however, they battle chronic diseases and sometimes pass away quickly post-retirement, never enjoying what they saved and sacrificed for.

Many of us find it difficult to retire largely because the human brain experiences physiological changes during our careers. Not to get too *sciencey*, but our brain constantly creates connections between neurons. We begin to form synapses that reflect the way we live our lives, that mirror who we actually are in the real world and how we operate to ensure our brain is synced and in a position to keep guaranteeing our survival.[10]

If we run on an operating system for years on end based on a 9-5 routine, stability "guaranteed," and wrangle in office politics, our brain literally adapts to that lifestyle. The more time we behave this way, the stronger these connections become in our minds, and the more we rely on that lifestyle—until our true self vanishes. When we reach our late fifties or sixties and finally embark upon our personal journey, we find ourselves desperate to return to work, because that's what we have known all our adulthood. Work becomes our core identity.

Even if few of us could maintain that other part of ourselves, our bodies, minds, and souls age. We can't run those marathons we so dearly kept on our bucket list but never had the time to pursue or fulfill "because of work." We never took our kids to a baseball game—or if we did, we were constantly answering emails "because of work." We never embraced our loved ones and gifted them with our presence "because of work." We never took that month-long trip to Asia with our partner "because of work." What we so desperately wanted to enjoy just when we achieved freedom is now impossible—our knees give out, our bodies become fragile, and our souls are not as illuminated as they once were. Our creative soul vanishes into a void.

To fight against this, we must remember that it is already late in the game. Game time is now. The countdown has started, and there is no restart button to press.

Go eat those Lucky Charms—and make sure it is stashed in your kitchen so you don't wake up in the middle of the night with a sudden existential craving for sugar that intertwines with existential questions about life.

But remember that, even if they taste like a golden treasure, they are just cornflakes.

The After Class Bell Rung, and the Real Lessons Began

While in college, my cousin had a revelation about what truly matters in life. He didn't learn it from a book or a course, he learned it through the firsthand experience of his philosophy teacher.

Professor Josh (we'll keep his real name a secret) had a core purpose as a teacher: to mold his students minds so they had a uniquely subjective perspective on how to live a meaningful life outside the classroom. Josh would be the kind of teacher who *really taught* when the after class bell rang, and his students— including my cousin—would sometimes skip their next class to have a deep talk about life beyond the classroom—and about their prospective paths after graduation.

My cousin has a deep, exploratory mind. This would fuel his participation in Philosophy 201. One day, as he was driving to class, he noticed he was carrying some additional existential angst, and couldn't wait until the bell rang so the *real class* of Professor Josh would start. He approached Josh and told him that, as graduation was nearing, he started the application process for consultant jobs. He shared his anxiety about working, and perhaps sacrificing all of his present time for a mythical better tomorrow. One of his biggest concerns was sacrificing his true colors for any career path just to amass wealth, like countless previous generations had done before him.

Josh listened closely, maybe closer than ever before.

He often responded to his students' questions with metaphors drawn from the works of great philosophers like Marcus Aurelius or Seneca, offering the profound insights that we all deeply seek.

This time he decided to share the following personal story.

When he was in his twenties, Professor Josh wrote himself a letter; he wrote that whatever he did in life it must have soul and depth, and he wouldn't sell his soul to a corporation or to an idea—not ever.

Professor Josh stored the letter in a box where, as time passed, it became a faded memory. Upon graduation, he began an amazing, successful career, immersing himself in significant diplomatic endeavors and international projects often related to a corporate and political setting. Although he found success in the external world, he had forgotten about the letter he wrote to himself all those years ago.

Many years later, as he was sorting through old boxes, he found the letter. When he read that same letter at sixty years old, his eyes began to water. He felt as if he had betrayed his youthful self, and as he read through it entirely, he broke down. He remembered what he felt during his twenties, but only began to explore that side of himself decades later when he thought he had more time.

He told my cousin that when we make decisions at critical moments in our lives, those choices will define how we shape our time on Earth. He asked my cousin, "Are you crafting a meaningful life not only for others, but for yourself?"

"If not," he said, "**The Time is Now** to explore this question, and design a life that will fulfill you deep within your soul." He encouraged my cousin to stick to his guns, make sure he happens to life and life doesn't happen to him, always stay alert to career-building temptations, and trust his intuitive powers.

Professor Josh demands for us to not be another statistic. Instead, he tells us to be brave and ask ourselves the following profound, intimate questions.

• What is a life well lived by my definition?

• What makes my soul burn with passion?

• How can I stay true to myself in a world that demands conformity?

• Am I genuinely crafting a meaningful life—not only for others but for myself?

Pause and Ponder: Chapter Two

• Do I feel a compulsion or need to achieve specific things in life? Why?

• Are my life goals genuinely a natural expression of who I am, or have they been influenced by external expectations?

• Are the dreams and ambitions I pursue truly my own, or have they been shaped by others' desires?

• Am I living life fully and intentionally, or simply going through the motions on autopilot?

• If I had only one year left to live, would I choose to continue doing what I am currently doing with my life?

• What steps can I take now to start making a meaningful impact in the world? When will I begin this journey?

3

THE LAYERED LATER

It costs a lot to be wealthy. And I ain't talking about the money.

— PAUL PORTESI

Our modern narrative tells us that accumulating wealth—hoarding as much as we can—is the ultimate pathway to freedom. In principle, this idea is absolutely spot on, but only if you have enough "Fuck You" Money. This is the kind of wealth that allows you to live untethered, free from obligations to anyone or anything that doesn't align with your true path.

But here's the trap: the pursuit of "Fuck You" Money can easily morph into Fuck You, Money. When we obsessively hoard wealth, we risk falling into the deferred life plan—delaying our true calling to chase digits in a bank account. We convince ourselves that once we've saved enough, we'll finally be free to honor our passions and live fully. But often, that time never comes. We've tied ourselves not to freedom, but to the money itself.

Of course, money is a necessity. You need it to take care of yourself and your family, to provide stability and security. But I'd like you to be aware of how easy it is to fall into the trap of believing you need *all* the money you could ever dream of before you're allowed to pursue your passion.

Sam Altman, founder of OpenAI, an AI research and deployment company, critiques the "deferred life plan"[1] prevalent in Silicon Valley during an interview. He notes the common tendency among tech professionals to set ambitious financial goals in the short term, like making a hundred million dollars in five years, with the intent of pursuing their true passions afterward. Altman argues that this approach seldom succeeds because it lacks genuine commitment to either immediate financial gain or long-term passion projects, such as building rockets.

The notion of delaying our true desires in favor of immediate financial security often leads to a lack of fulfillment and engagement, which can be transparent to others and ultimately hinder our progress.

When we pursue financial freedom on a deferred life plan, we must remember the leprechaun's journey and the disappointment he encountered at the end of his road—empty cornflakes that may resemble gold. What we don't see in the leprechaun's journey, however, is the emotional toll he endured while blindly chasing the ultimate prize.

We only focus on the observable: his arrival at the destination.

Paul Portesi, a deep thinker who shares his ideas via X said:

> It's never the money cost but the emotional cost that's the most expensive. Sometimes no amount will cover the painful emotional drawdown. Most of the time, the most

costly ain't about the money. No, there's no overdraft protection for the emotional cost.[2]

In other words, when we embark on a blind journey for a given period of time towards amassing any kind of wealth, we overlook the emotional cost of this path, and this ends up being the most expensive receipt.

We keep the money, but we also retain the emotion. We keep the pain.

We keep the pain of living a deferred life plan; the pain of knowing we are delaying the pursuit of our true calling. The pain of delaying our exploration of our own humanity, and of others.

We keep the pain of refusing to listen to our hearts.

The deferred life plan is quite paradoxical because it makes so much sense rationally, and because it is a strategy designed to *protect us*. At least, that's what we think this path is doing.

It is also paradoxical because the intention is to allow yourself to have the means necessary to explore your creative potential. Not now, though. Later.

What haunts me, and might haunt you, is that the laters always come *later*. This is what I call the Layered Later: We peel back this onion of *laters* just to find more layers of *laters* waiting for us. We might end up spending decades peeling back the laters and when we finally get to the very last one, we may find ourselves exhausted from peeling back all of these laters so we just forgo pursuing our hearts.

The *later* never arrives.

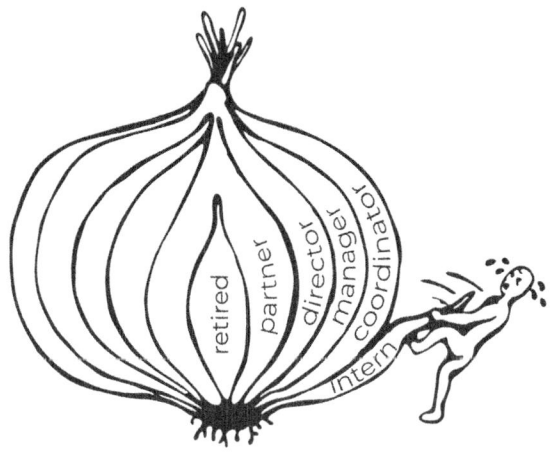

In one survey, a staggering seventy-seven percent of respondents would sacrifice their personal life to achieve some career success.[3] Yet, nine out of ten people regret rushing into a career choice early in their lives.[4]

Regardless of the lies we try to tell ourselves, there is a deep intuitive feeling that tells us money will never beat having good health, family, and time.

In the year 2023, a viral video circulated the internet in which people on the street were approached with the question, "If given a chance, would you take ten million dollars today?" Of course, all of them said "yes" immediately.[5] The catch, however, was the second question—they would get the money but not wake up tomorrow.

Immediately, all the interviewees said, "Absolutely not."

Such an extreme example sheds light on a truth we all know but don't want to accept: *No amount of money will ever be worth more than our time.* There is no price we can put on the time we sacrifice for money. Yet, in practice, two out of three Americans feel disconnected from their jobs, but many of them have chosen the fancy title with the huge salary.

Of course, my intention is not to demonize money or wealth in any way, as I know they are powerful resources to grow as individuals and are compounding forces that can bring prosperity to many.

But I bet you all the money in the world right now that you would give *anything* to go back in time to when you were younger; to relieve a memory, or have one more moment with a loved one who may have passed. I know I would.

Many of us who decide to take the path of career growth with the goal of maximizing wealth instead of pursuing those passionate creative projects we have in mind have a tingling sensation in the back of our brains that signals our inevitable discontent in later years. We rationalize the decision as a logical stepping stone toward actually having the resources to invest our time into our creative passions. We repress our creative potential and become hypnotized by the conventional mantra of "money first, enjoyment later," leading us to a deferred state of being—perhaps for all our lives.

But emotions relating to pursuing our passions—the things that truly motivate us and give us joy—remain latent throughout our lives.

Those emotions factor into every decision we make, and they charge a fee that society does not include in our net worth.

That realization is a sobering, tough-love reflection we all need to understand and internalize, along with the knowledge that time is our most valuable asset.

Ask yourself, if given the choice to earn a trillion dollars today but only live for another year, would you take that deal?

Ask yourself, if you would take a trillion dollars today in exchange for becoming depressed, lonely, and bitter—losing touch with who you truly are—throughout your life, would you take that deal?

Now, ask yourself, if offered the choice between fame, reputation, and wealth, or following your heart, nurturing relationships, and guarding your time, what would you choose?

If given the chance to wear a mask all your life, or embark on your journey to discover your true self, what would you choose?

Masks and Mirrors: Surrendering Your True Self for "Success"

> The distance between the mask and the true self is the distance between the real and the ideal.
>
> — *CARL JUNG*

Jim Carrey, one of the funniest people on Earth, starred in The Mask as Stanley Ipkiss, a man living a monotonous, colorless life. When Stanley finds a green mask, he transforms into an eccentric, charismatic hero who radiates confidence and seduces the love of his life, Tina Carlyle. Over time, Stanley realizes the mask's true power—it brings success and influence but at the cost of his essence, moral compass, and authenticity. The mask becomes harder to remove each time he wears it, symbolizing how societal pressures push us to adopt façades of wealth and status, distancing us from our true selves. Ultimately, Stanley learns that embracing his authentic identity is all he needs.

As the brilliant Chris Williamson, the host of the Modern Wisdom Podcast and previous guest on my podcast states,[6]

"People sacrifice the thing they want (happiness) for the thing which is supposed to get it (success). We give up happiness to achieve success so that we can finally be happy when we achieve enough success. Backward."[7]

In other words, many of us already have found happiness by doing what we love. However, we have been socialized to believe that we must sacrifice for a long time to become successful enough to unburden ourselves and *eventually* engage again in what makes us happy. That doesn't make sense, and many of us are finally awakening to this backward idea.

I, too, fell victim to wearing a mask—identifying with it until I realized the game I was playing was changing me, and the gap between the mask and my true self began to close making it harder and harder to distinguish between them. My true sense of self was losing its battle with the façade. I was becoming the façade.

I must note that I was lucky enough to only play the game for less than five years before I began to feel how much I was changing—and losing.

Now imagine playing a game that you don't love for over thirty years!

No one alive could wear a mask and simultaneously have a genuine sense of self. Eventually, the longer we play, the faster the façade becomes the self, and the self becomes the façade.

Oftentimes when we ask our elderly loved ones about their most significant regrets, their answers include not doing what they love, not taking that risk that always burned deep within their hearts, and choosing money over investing in family time.

For many, and myself, masks become defense mechanisms. We believe we can only accomplish remarkable feats when we wear them. This can also mute our rawest emotions, providing a false sense of relief that we are doing 'great' on paper while our true feelings remain unexamined. The problem is the more we dismiss these feelings, the more we need the mask to defend ourselves against the emotions we want to avoid.

The mask itself becomes a coping strategy against *really* staring ourselves in the mirror and seeing ourselves for who we are. That might be too painful. When we neglect our true colors for so long, even entertaining the idea of experiencing self-examination can be traumatizing, so we would rather wear the mask than experience the pain of truth.

We would rather dissociate ourselves *from ourselves* than embrace who we truly are.

As a result, we witness a direct impact on the way we live our lives —fragmented lives, putting work in one box, isolating our personal affairs in another, and desperately trying to find a "work-life balance" rather than integrating our lives' various aspects to achieve harmony and equilibrium.

This compartmentalization of life inevitably leads to the fragmentation of the self. Of ourselves.

We buy into the idea that our true selves are somehow a liability. We start to smooth out every unique, messy, and imperfect trait we have, just to fit in. It's like when people turn to Botox or plastic surgery, trying to erase the lines of experience or reshape their bodies to meet some external standard—hiding the features that make them stand out. We bend ourselves to blend in, to go unnoticed, to avoid making anyone uncomfortable...to become literal squares. But those so-called imperfections—the lines, the curves, the quirks—are exactly what make us human, what make us whole. By stripping them away, we lose touch with our authentic selves, and in doing so, we lose the very essence of what makes us unique.

We have the whole concept of life backwards. We should not strangle our authentic selves, our happiness, in exchange for conventional, bland, and lifeless—conventional—success.

Worse still, when we play these games, we realize that when we arrive at 'success,' there is nothing tangible to redeem in exchange —only emptiness. Although we've "made it," the chase never ends because the layered promises of fulfillment were illusions all along. This ties back to the idea of the Layered Later: the belief that sacrificing our genuine selves in the present will lead to a better life later. But the mask, much like the deferred life plan, takes control over time. It blurs our vision, making it harder to remove, until we no longer recognize ourselves. The best we can do is to live authentically now, refusing to sacrifice who we are for a life built on false ideals of what success should look like.

The Trap of Winning

Modern success can be compared to becoming a great game-player. Most of us can adapt to modern games easily: the role of the corporate genius, the intellectual writer, the politician, the great student, the successful businessman.

I feel deep within myself that I can confidently win and adapt to any role in the modern workplace because it's less about working and more about role-playing—more about the mask. The problem is that when we play these games, we stand at the risk of actually winning them.

Ram Dass, a prominent spiritual teacher and former academic, once epitomized conventional success with an impressive array of academic and material achievements. At the peak of his academic career, he had seemingly achieved it all—from prestigious appointments at Harvard and visiting professorships to an enviable collection of luxury items and desirable lifestyle perks. Yet, despite these accolades and possessions that signaled success, he ultimately recognized that his accomplishments were part of playing a well-orchestrated "game." In his words, his conventional success only boiled down to the fact that he was "a very good game player."[8]

Ram Dass was spot on. He succeeded in life because of his ability to be a good game player; he followed the rules of the game and reaped the rewards of wealth, prestige, and success. He had access to the world's most exclusive and important research institutions, such as Harvard and Yale, and owned a motorcycle and an airplane.

Time showed Ram Dass that the material possessions and the perks of being a great game player came with a cost: his true self.

Ram Dass had everything he thought he wanted, but he was miserable. He was playing the game, but he wasn't really in the game.

What a profound message. Ram Dass played the game but never felt part of the game. He was living a life of success, but he was empty inside. He felt like he was going through the motions.

There are several parallels to his story and mine (maybe not the scuba diving, or being a renowned Harvard psychologist, or owning an airplane). My role-playing abilities rewarded me in a material sense, and every time I role-played, I felt depleted. I was also playing the game, but was never a part of it.

If I had continued to play a game I didn't feel a part of, everything that would have emerged from that insincere path; all my efforts would have been based on complacency and deception—toward others and myself—and a loss of integrity. Even if I had accomplished greatness, it would still have felt rotten inside.

Ram Dass' journey to his "this-really-isn't-it" realization led to the courageous act of leaving behind an outstanding reputation, enviable wealth, and a great career. He became one of the world's most impactful gurus, helping millions in their spiritual journeys, all while he experienced life from the most genuine space within himself.

While the upsides of playing a game that is not yours are indeed rewarding, they will always pale in comparison to building your own game. The rewards of deeply understanding the façade and the dangers of getting swallowed up in personal gain and corn-flakes are infinite.

That realization is the epitome of the true definition of "success."

While our minds are lured by materialism and opportunity, our souls receive immeasurable nourishment from the intangible. To awaken to that truth, we must eliminate everything we are *not*: We must remove our masks—who we thought we must be—to become who we truly are. We must also understand the underlying mechanisms, such as our evolutionary code, that drive us to pursue acquisition and accumulation through conventional means—like mask-wearing.

Pause and Ponder: Chapter Three

• Am I prioritizing external validation and societal expectations over my own happiness and well-being?

• What steps can I take to integrate my passions and creative pursuits into my current lifestyle, rather than waiting for a distant future?

• What do I perceive as the risks and benefits of following a deferred life plan?

4

BIO-WIRED TO HUNT SUCCESS

The only way to truly win the game of status is to not play.

— NAVAL RAVIKANT

Chasing status and prestige are deeply embedded in our biological blueprint. But what exactly is it about our biology, evolutionary blueprint, and heritage that drives us into playing these worldly games of external success? Why does it seem that we are all attracted, at least on an unconscious level and from an evolutionary standpoint, to playing these kinds of games?

Our evolutionary code, coupled with our social pressures, has made its best effort to adapt to the modern lifestyle and drives us to desire things that allow us to fulfill our biological needs—the two most important of which are social bonding and reproduction.[1]

The deep-seated social bonding we crave stems from an extensive, million-year-old evolutionary code. This instinctual drive is not a choice but a crucial aspect of our survival mechanism inherited across generations. As social creatures, our ancestors depended on group cohesion and approval for protection, resource sharing, and reproduction—making social bonds vital for their survival. Today, this manifests in our desire for approval from loved ones, community and broader society. However, the paradox emerges when the pursuit of approval leads to feelings of inadequacy, as our need for acceptance can sometimes make us feel less accepted and more isolated.

In modern times, many people look for a 9-5 job, but our evolutionary code is not designed to withstand that lifestyle. For the vast majority of human history, our ancestors thrived in dynamic, flexible environments. Instead of regimented schedules and repetitive tasks, early humans lived as hunters, gatherers, and community builders, engaging in varied, physically and mentally stimulating activities.

Modern 9-to-5 jobs, on the other hand, often prioritize monotony and routine over creativity and spontaneity. Studies in evolutionary psychology suggest that such structured, sedentary lifestyles can lead to chronic stress, decreased mental well-being, and physical health problems because they conflict with our innate need for movement, connection, and exploration.[2] We must leverage the perks of living in modernity—one of the most peaceful eras in recorded history—to look inward and find our authentic path instead of giving ourselves away to the inertia of modern games.

However, we believe that by staying in our lane and working at a regular job—being part of a big pack—we guarantee our survival. Thus, our drive is to search for a comfortable place that sells all the above.

Our priority instinctually becomes self-*protection*, not self-*awareness*.

The dangerous aspect of our focus is that we do not yield the dividends we envisioned. More than 80 percent of Gen Z and Millennials experience heightened levels of depression and anxiety throughout their careers[3], thus reducing their chances of survival and reproduction in the long run. In fact, the fertility crisis that our world now witnesses in real-time is one of the most overlooked existential dilemmas we face.

I hosted Dr. Sarah Martins da Silva for an interview[4], a fertility specialist recognized for her research in 2019 and named as one of the most inspiring and influential women from around the world by BBC 100 women, who shared with me a troubling statistic: Studies show there is a global fifty percent decline in sperm counts in men over the previous sixty years.[5] If you extend the line of sperm counts for Western men, it hits zero in 2045. Research has shown that there is a link between depression and infertility.[6] Additionally, women with a history of depression are twice as likely to experience infertility.[7]

Guess which generations have had the greatest fertility issues? Millennials and Gen Z.[8]

Of course, there is an endless list of potential reasons that cause such a sharp, existential reproductive decline aside from depression and anxiety. However, experiencing these two regularly and consistently does not help our reproductive cause.

Most of our social activities tie in with finding a potential mate.[9] To signal reproductive value, we seek high-status or high-paying jobs that fill this desire but also can leave us feeling purposeless. This idea was explored extensively in *The Status Game*[10] by the brilliant author and previous guest on my podcast,[11] Will Storr, in which he offers insights into the reasons behind humanity's desire to play status games (which, he argues, we can never win).

His opening line is, "Life is a game." But within the game of life, we play multiple other games through our evolution, including status games which, in a sense, have ensured our survival to this day. The rules of the game are ingrained into our DNA, so it is easy for us to understand the following concept: the more we climb the status ladder, the more access we have to resources, respect, and mating opportunities.

This idea, Will suggests, comes from research done by Professor David Buss, evolutionary psychologist at the University of Texas at Austin, and previous guest on my show.[12] He found that men who had a higher status 'invariably' had more access to wealth and mating partners in over 180 pre-modern societies. While this study focused primarily on men, research also suggests that status plays a significant role across gender identities. For women, the drive for status often relates to securing resources, social influence, and opportunities, reflecting a universal human motive across cultures, genders, and personalities.[13] These ideas are very straightforward. The higher you are on the status ladder, the better off you will be.[14]

I'd like to reference 21 Savage, a well-known rapper, who brilliantly captures the essence of the status game that pervades the modern world. In one song, he starkly states:

> This world's all about money and pussy. And you need to figure that out. Once you figure that out, you'll be better off in life.[15]

As you can see, 21 Savage has eloquently summarized the whole evolutionary blueprint that drives us to achieve higher levels of social status in modern times. The modern world moves around money and mating; the more money we have, the more we gain access to reproductive opportunities. We can also admire famous Canadian rapper, Drake, for his song, "Successful" featuring Lil Wayne and Trey Songz, and its ability to capture our evolutionary blueprint in just one chorus:

> I want the money (Money), money and the cars, Cars and the clothes (Clothes), the hoes, I suppose, I just wanna be, I just wanna be successful[16]

As it turns out, 21 Savage, Drake, Lil Wayne and Trey Songz could be better social scientists than *actual* social scientists.

One study titled, "Why do men seek status? Fitness payoffs to dominance and prestige," suggests that their lyrics have more truth about us than we think. Researchers observed a positive correlation between a man's status and the number of descendants he has.[17]

In a small Amerindian society, they found that dominant men—those who are more likely to win physical confrontations—have higher fertility rates within their marriages. Also, it was found that prestigious men, meaning those who wield more influence within the community, not only have more children but also experience lower child mortality rates.

Another insight was that both types of high-status men receive support from allies and respect from rivals, and prestigious men often marry women who start families at younger ages, contributing to their greater reproductive success; both dominant and prestigious men were found to have more children inside and outside of marriage, showing that the quest for status is linked to long-term reproductive advantages.[18]

Another study conducted among the pastoralist Yomut Turkmen of Iran was one of the first to quantitatively show a link between a man's material wealth and the number of offspring he has, with wealthier men having more children.[19]

To seek further contextual insight into what the famous *social science rappers* said, we can look to American psychologist Geoffrey Miller. In his book, *The Mating Mind*, Miller argues that our brains are deeply wired for a hunter-gatherer lifestyle, which has caused an array of problems in our modern, urbanized societies. He states that life during pre-modern times was about scanning for potential threats like a lion chasing humans as prey. Miller asserts we are constantly on alert for threats, even when none are present.[20]

In modernity, this evolutionary need to constantly—some may say even obsessively—scan our surroundings can lead to anxiety and stress. Additionally, Miller points out that our brains are designed to constantly seek out new sources of food and mates; thus, we embark on worldly pursuits to achieve these goals. In his words,

> "In modern market economies people put a high value on wealth indicators during courtship. This can be rational, given the range of goods and services that money can buy, and the difference it can make to one's quality of life. As Thorstein Veblen, an American economist and sociologist known for his critique of capitalism and for coining the term "conspicuous consumption,"argued a century ago, modern culture is basically a system of conspicuous consumption in which people demonstrate their wealth by wasting it on luxuries."[21]

In modernity, we don't need to kill a lion or bring home a giant boar for dinner to prove our worthiness as high status individuals —we can just get a six-figure job, share it on LinkedIn, and post a selfie with our brand new car and achieve the same result: We are deemed high-status, high-income individuals. Thus, more people pay attention to who we are and begin intriguing themselves with our worthiness as potential mating partners, friends, or allies in order for us to obtain the same results.

Nowadays, we play "the status game" to its most extreme extent, and we do so unquestioningly for two reasons: It is embedded in our nature, and it has become a highly addictive and *commoditized* game. Again, as Miller argued in *The Mating Mind*, modernity is basically a market system where we use our wealth to spend conspicuously on luxury goods to signal high mate value.[22]

In the end, I suppose, we all just wanna be, we just wanna be successful.

The College Games

> Colleges have become status-stamping machines.
>
> — NAVAL RAVIKANT

Have you ever thought about how a prestigious college gets you to apply to their undergraduate programs? On every single website, if you go to their "About" page, they strategically record their rankings and compare them to other college programs. In doing so, these institutions are playing the status game themselves! Truly unescapable.

For example, they might take pride in being Top Ten in the United States for research, education outcomes, and low acceptance rates. What these three statistics do is they appeal to our status-seeking evolutionary code that salivates when we envision our affiliation with a top-ten institution that guarantees a high-paying job post-graduation and our acceptance, having competed against hundreds of thousands of other applicants.

We are falsely led to believe that an opportunity like this is the *only secured path* so we can amass us more resources and mating opportunities, combined with many other evolutionarily driven nudges that tempt us to not think twice about wasting upwards of $250,000 in four years in studies. These methods are effective because they supersede the rational mind—even while blabbing out statistics—and speak directly to our status-seeking instincts.

My dream was to attend University of Miami, and now I am thankful I didn't go there as it meant that I would have been in debt *before even starting my career,* owing the university over $50,000 or more. At the time of writing, the yearly tuition to attend "UM" has reached $90,000.[23]

Moreover, almost every college takes pride in advertising their notable alumni, saying things like, "We were home to Barack Obama, Meghan Markle, and Tim Cook." Instantly, we feel that we can become higher-status individuals by association because we associate the success of these figures with their college education, prompting our minds to believe that the identical achievement will apply to us. Ultimately, we can brag about attending the same college as the 44th President of the United States, leading us to believe we now rank higher on the status ladder than before.

Of course, these colleges do not articulate what 21 Savage so brilliantly and eloquently rapped about, but they are carefully—or, on second thought, not so discreetly—saying the exact same thing: "If you get accepted into our institution, you'll have access to status, and can potentially obtain more resources and more mating opportunities."

In short, you'll fulfill your dreams of becoming successful.

For a lucky few, the investment does pay off in a material sense without inflicting any cost to their future finances or quality of living. But for most people, this status-seeking game has cost them at least twenty years of their life—and up to forty-five years— paying off their student loans.

The student loan debt crisis in the United States is staggering. Researchers Mary Beal, Mary O. Borg, and Harriet A. Stranahan found that there are over 44 million borrowers and a total debt exceeding $1.3 trillion, making it the second-largest consumer debt category after mortgages. Over $32 billion of this debt is currently in default, indicating the financial strain it places on borrowers. The average student loan debt for graduates in 2016 was over $37,000, with an alarming two million borrowers owing over $100,000.[24]

Only 23 percent of students from families with incomes below $30,000 graduate without debt, compared to 62 percent of students from families with incomes over $100,000.[25] In for-profit institutions, a high percentage of graduates across all income levels end up with debts exceeding $30,500. Specifically, 64 percent of dependent students from families earning $60,000 to $99,999 and 37 percent from families earning $30,000 to $59,999 graduate with substantial debt.[26]

Okay, that was a lot of numbers. Let's carry on.

As a result, many graduates experience depression post-gradua-tion, not because they explored their true interests and passions in college, but because they pursued status-driven paths that left them unfulfilled. The promise of higher status quickly fades once they confront the stark reality of their situation: decades of debt, uncertainty about their careers—possibly without a job at all—and the realization that, in the end, no one truly cared about their "prestigious" major.[27]

For millions of Americans, the only guarantee they have upon graduation is a monthly charge—with interest—for decades. I'm not saying higher education is a waste of time in its entirety. However, we must acknowledge that colleges and universities play a significant role in perpetuating the status game. Too often, people choose a college based on its prestige rather than how well it aligns with their passions, values, and interests.

Educational institutions use predatory strategies to attract individuals to attend their institutions. Since we're programmed to desire status and reward those with more prominent status, bad actors exploit a positive evolutionary code to extract the rewards themselves; when reality hits, these institutions, alongside some of our politicians and many in the corporate world that promise evolutionary-alluring opportunities such as access to "high-paying jobs and a vast network of successful people to connect with," remain in power while good people with good intentions and true virtuosity risk falling behind and being forgotten. Again, these promises, while enticing, frequently mask an underlying reality: they benefit the institutions and corporations more than the individuals they claim to serve.

I know, this just took a rather serious turn—as it should!

Once you know how many bad actors are exploiting our evolutionary code for their benefit, you begin to see the game for what it is: a rigged-attempt to appeal to your most instinctual desires. The end result is that you play a game you can never win, and you become so emotionally and biologically attached to the game that you become dependent on it indefinitely. Then, you begin to normalize your feelings of depression, anxiety, and disappointment. These begin to be perceived as part of our natural laws of existence.

The good side of all this is that you now have access to examine the deeper game that is playing out—a game that has been in the making for millions of years and now finds itself in control of people with rather bad intentions who want to extract everything you have and sell you a false promise that strips away your most valuable assets: your time, your creativity, and your life force.

When you notice how our evolutionary code drives most of our actions, you paradoxically find yourself in a position to remove yourself from the game and actually begin to discover your true self on your own terms.

Once we see the status game for what it truly is, the game shifts completely: Those who become the most attractive people are the ones who dare to stop playing a rigged game, follow their own personal journey, and are willing to explore their authentic selves without giving into the inertia of worldly games. The challenge here is that this practice is not taught in a healthy, productive way; most people are programmed to follow a recipe for life, and that instruction almost always fails to live up to its promise, making us feel a deep sense of despair, as if we settled for an inauthentic path.

In truth, we live in the best of times where we can see beyond our *pre-programmed* beliefs and evolutionary code to explore the deeper layers of our endeavors. That insight puts us in a solid position to reevaluate our paths by understanding the forces that drive us to make certain decisions. Inevitably, that realization places us on the highest rung of the status ladder, as we no longer abide by predatory rules that others impose as if they were immutable universal laws.

Now that you see the game for what it truly is, you can create your own game with your own rules. In that sense, you are the ruler of the world—the most resourceful, attractive mating partner anyone can ever find.

Slowly but surely, when more of us catch the *catch* of the worldly game society plays, those politicians who virtue-signal, those peers who desperately need accolades to prove their worthiness, and those institutions who prey on our deepest desires, will be removed from the status game altogether.

Detach yourself from the need to boast your worthiness based on who you know, what you do, and what you earn, and realize that is the ultimate power move; now, as you have become boundless and released from the golden, *evolutionarily driven* chains you were locked in, go ahead and create your own world and build your own reality driven by your true self, not by narcissistic needs.

In a world filled with hypocrisy and deceit, playing your own game is almost a moral duty with existential consequences; being a virtuous individual with a strong sense of integrity, as Nathaniel Branden wrote in his book Six Pillars of Self-Esteem, is akin to being a modern superhero.[28]

Give yourself time to let the answers arise from within you—not from what the Ivy League schools preach, or the highly acclaimed authors suggest you should do. Just give yourself some space, and the answers will manifest because *you are the key* to winning the game of life. You are the key to becoming successful.

Real Virtue in the 21st Century

> If you're playing a game for applause, you're playing the wrong game.
>
> — *NAVAL* RAVIKANT

Most of us who play status games try to "shine our armor" by boasting on our credentials. When people introduce themselves by saying, *"Hello, I'm Alex, and I graduated from Stanford Summa Cum Laude with honors and the Presidential Award for Best Student,"* those who meet this individual may feel a slight sense of cringe and quickly identify him as someone trying to use their "medals" as an armor to climb the ladder of success. That kind of introduction and self-identification almost always backfires and functions as a quick turnoff because most people can sense when others are virtue signaling without actually being virtuous.

In The *Status Game*, Will Storr portrays "the virtue game" as the reward of status "to players who are conspicuously dutiful, obedient and moralistic."[29] In other words, virtue signaling can provide great returns in gaining status since the price to play is relatively cheap, and the opportunities to showcase our obedience and accolades are endless. We can leverage social media to post about our awards, and our social circle gets to see them. At that point, there is a tangible possibility that hundreds of thousands of potential allies, mating partners, etc., could see our worthiness as higher-status individuals with just the click of a mouse or touchscreen, without inflicting physical costs, such as the battlefield injuries that we may have received in the past.

The game of virtue has very few entry barriers, and very few actually take the time to prove whether or not someone is virtuous after posting their accomplishments or good deeds. The moment someone posts about their new job, their opinion on a certain contentious topic, or boasts about their awards, we falsely believe we have all the necessary, face-value "evidence" to prove that they are higher on the status ladder than before. But, in reality, it should reveal the exact opposite: Those who boast the most about their virtues tend to be, in fact, the least virtuous people. For example, research has found that individuals who engage in public displays of moral outrage, a form of virtue signaling, are often motivated by a desire to enhance one's social standing rather than a commitment to moral principles.[30]

Let's dive into a small "side quest" here: Do you know which category of individuals exploit this easily played game? Many of our politicians. If you scroll through any world leader's social media accounts or pay attention to what they say, you will notice a pattern. They are experts in virtue signaling, and instead of acting good for the sake of doing so, everything becomes a photo-opp. Many modern politicians know they can earn our votes not because of who they are but because of what they signal. Surprisingly—and frighteningly—it just so happens that these individuals dominate the political landscape.

Take LinkedIn, for example. LinkedIn is an excellent platform for professionals. It can connect you with your dream job and help expand your social and professional network. But many people use the platform to play a status game.

By now, we understand humans are very good at playing social games. We are literally designed that way. These games tend to be hierarchical. The haves and have-nots are clearly defined, and our evolutionary blueprint appears in every game we play. We cannot escape the status games.

Within the social hierarchies of most societies, the wealthy, powerful, or well-connected are typically at the top, while the poor, disenfranchised, powerless, or marginalized are usually at the bottom. Invariably, we encounter a hierarchy of power and authority in most workplaces. Those at the top have more power, authority, and influence than those at the bottom. Most of the time the house of cards is based on seniority.

Our instinct to reproduce ties in with status and can drive us to do crazy things to prove our value as mates. In other species, this is very evident and well documented. Peacocks, for example, generally have long tails, which have caused time-honored discussion among evolutionary psychologists and biologists, including Professor David Buss, who opines that peacocks have long tails due to sexual selection. That is, peahens choose to mate with males that have luminescent tails.[31]

In the human realm, we, too, have our own "tails" to signal our mate value.

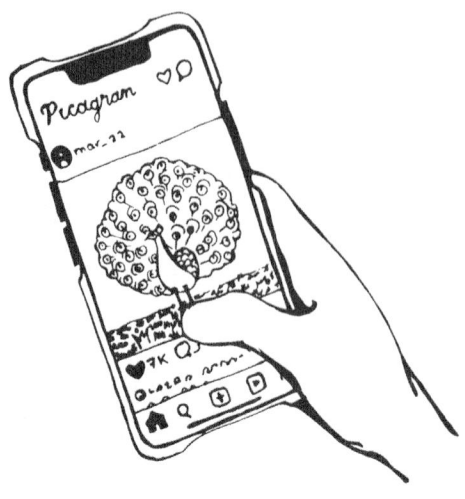

We possess qualitative traits that qualify as higher-value mating indicators: Is the male hard-working? Does he have characteristics that improve his odds of accessing resources? Does he have potential? Is he ambitious?

In our present social context—a world increasingly technological with our definition of a "stable job" at its core—we perceive intellectual talent as a highly valued trait for mating. Thousands of years ago, our ancestors in hunter-gatherer societies defined priority or value in the primal mating market as hunting or killing mammoths, bringing food to the table. In modern Western Societies, we don't need to kill a mammoth to prove our mating value. We can get a high-paying job that does the same trick.

Those who perform professional, desk, managerial, or administrative work apparently have higher mating value. These kinds of careers are typically highly paid compared to other types of work, and those who engage in them tend to have higher educational achievements. These activities also signal qualitative traits such as intelligence, ambition, and potential to acquire more resources in the long run.

And how does LinkedIn enter the evolutionary discussion room? This platform is being used to signal our value—to potential mates and to other peers in our network—and our worthiness as high-status individuals.

When we scroll on LinkedIn, we tend to find all these posts that say, "I'm excited to join this prestigious company," and "It took a lot of hard work, tears, and long nights, but I can finally say I obtained my master's degree." These messages seem to be virtue signaling that instantly gives you access to the hierarchy, where you realize you're climbing the ladder. Unconsciously and consciously, the message creates a feeling, from the perspective of someone not in that position, that signals, "Hey, they're playing the game better than me—even if I didn't study finance. Wow! They're consultants at Mckinsey."

And how does all this rant about our evolutionary code connect with our time on Earth and choosing a career that, while offering potentially great returns on investment financially and reputationally, can make us unhappy? Well, it reveals some hidden motives behind our desire to climb the corporate ladder; becoming someone who is great at playing modern status games can become a great way to obtain prestige.

On a deeper level, however, we can fall under the illusion that we are playing these status games because we like them. But in reality, many of us are waiting to get that master's degree, be hired at

Mckinsey, earn that diploma, just to be able to boast about it and post it on LinkedIn. On a neurological level, we associate the satisfaction of our hard work with posting about our achievements on social media. In other words, we no longer get Dopamine and Serotonin—often referred to as the "feel good hormones"—when we engage in a difficult task. They are often secreted only *after* we post on LinkedIn. [32] In other *other* words, the rewarding sensation comes from the social validation received after sharing achievements online, rather than from the completion of difficult tasks themselves.

So many of us engage in this senseless chase for career success because we are wired to chase status. But deeper than that, our satisfaction arises from virtue signaling our achievements with our peers rather than deriving fulfillment from engaging in difficult activities. In short, we chase that white-collar job for the "likes," for what it represents, and to satisfy our evolutionary blueprint's demands in the most cost-effective way possible for our minds.

Once we understand how we are built to chase success, two insights emerge:

First, we can appreciate the reasons behind our motives and that knowledge sheds light on how absurdly funny some of our actions are: "Am I trying to get that job just for what it represents, and just to signal my worthiness so I can pass on my genes?"

I admit that, for me, some decisions have been unconsciously driven by this peacock desire.

Second, through these insights, we can see some of the deceptive techniques some use to signal virtuosity; next time you see a post on social media about someone tooting their own horn, ask yourself if that is true virtuosity or a deceptive strategy showing outstanding achievements at little to no cost.

When we understand the underpinnings of our nature, we have a better chance to reflect on what we truly want to do in life. Do we really want to spend thirty years of our lives proving our worthiness by playing status games, or can we engage in activities that give us fulfillment and, paradoxically, elevate our status?

Could we engage in a fulfilling activity that leads to climbing the ladder in the *absence* of our desire to climb the ladder? The answer is yes, because when we do things for the love of them, they feel like *play*. We are not bound by formality and rigid planning, and therefore what we do doesn't feel like work; our natural abilities are displayed in plain sight and are honest signals to others about our true worth; those who lean into their true selves rarely toot their own horn because their craft toots their horn on their behalf.

The highest signal of status is one that arises out of not seeking that status. However, if someone states that they don't play status games, they are among the people who play status games the most. The trick is to unbind ourselves from these games by accepting that we play them—as they are embedded in our DNA.

Naval Ravikant posted the following:

> "Two kinds of happiness: Worldly happiness is a reward from our evolutionary program. Get praise, money, drugs, sex. It busies the mind with cravings and anxiety. Internal happiness is a reward for being in the flow. Create, meditate, love, and play. It clears the mind and leaves us in peace."[33]

Our sense of happiness from our evolutionary code has been hijacked in modernity. It was once useful, allowing us to seek novelty and adventure. The feel-good hormones, such as Dopamine (a neurotransmitter released in the brain, involved in learning, motivation, and memory) is triggered when we find ourselves in a new environment that demands us to pay attention to our surroundings, or when we learn something new.

In my interview with Anna Lembke, addiction specialist and psychiatrist at Stanford University School of Medicine, she described how one of the biggest misconceptions about Dopamine is that it's just a "pleasure" hormone.[34] In her words:

> "It is important to note that one of the misconceptions about Dopamine is that it is just part of getting high or feeling pleasure. This is an oversimplification, as Dopamine is also stimulated by novelty or new things in the environment, even if they are not necessarily pleasurable. Dopamine is a neurotransmitter that tells us to pay attention to what is going on right now."

Dopamine is part of our brain's reward system that incentivizes novelty. But in today's world, as Dr. Anna Lembke writes in her book, *Dopamine Nation: Finding Balance in an Age of Indulgence*, our technologies have hijacked our reward system and have deceived it into chasing instant gratification.[35]

During our interview, Dr. Lembke asserted that the algorithms have exploited our evolutionary code for their benefit:

> "...and of course, the internet exploits this wonderfully by continually suggesting to us through AI algorithms that have learned what we have liked before, but with a slightly novel twist to it. This engages our treasure-seeking function, which has us looking and looking and looking."

That is why when we scroll through LinkedIn, Instagram, or any other social media platform, we crave more and are filled with anxiety because it is never enough. We will never get enough praise from our post-boasting about how we got our master's diploma; we will never feel enough satisfaction from virtue signaling; we will never settle with just working hard and not posting. Our worldly happiness, driven by our evolutionary code, has been hijacked to the point where we cannot feel any satisfaction for the sake of engaging in novel, challenging endeavors. Instead, they must be signaled for our reward systems to *reward us.*

You may think I'm suggesting we drop out from worldly experiences altogether and embrace the idea of Naval's internal happiness, but I'm not. In fact, by opening our eyes to the truth of how our evolutionary code has not caught up with our modern lifestyles—and how many institutions, corporations, and some individuals are actively—and I mean *actively*—working to make sure our evolutionary blueprint works for them, we can enjoy worldly happiness without becoming a slave to it.

When we look within before posting our achievements, we would do well by asking ourselves the following existential-question-slash-rant:

"What if I am just posting to seek the praise from others, and perhaps the praise will never be enough to actually fulfill me, so this will lead me to continue playing these games (some of which I don't like) just because my reward system that once used to reward learning and novelty, is now hijacked and is making me virtue signal my accomplishments?

As a result, it might just fulfill me, but it never actually does. And what if I never get to experience actual, internal fulfillment from what I do in life because my reward systems have associated 'feeling good' with 'posting,' which always leaves me feeling anxious and craving more—rather than feeling good because I learned something new or learned a difficult lesson while engaging in an activity that fulfills me? Yet, I continue to post and intend to do so for the foreseeable future...

Why is that?"

Introspective reflection holds tremendous power; it frees us from the golden handcuffs of modernity—praise, virtue signaling—and opens the door to internal happiness. This type of happiness can form the foundation of a life built on love rather than anxiety and fear of missing out.

Our evolutionary code is brilliant—the product of millions of years that have enabled us to arrive at where we are now. I'm all about having worldly experiences, but these experiences must arise from our internal happiness more than from the desire for status.

Praise, sex, and money can emerge as byproducts of activities that foster connection, like engaging in flow, love, creation, and passion. These worldly experiences should not be *the ends* or *outcomes* we try to reach. In fact, that shouldn't even be on our radar. Instead, they should be what are called positive externalities —benefits that arise naturally from our creative nature and enhance our lives without being the primary goal.

The first step to achieving integration in the world comes from understanding our evolutionary desires; by integrating, I mean achieving harmony between these desires—such as the pursuit of status, community, and survival—and the deeper, often over-looked aspects of our human potential, including creativity, authenticity, and a sense of purpose. By having a glimpse into what mechanisms drive our motivations to play these modern status games, we can be free of them long before our brain boggles with endless anxiety and desperately craves more of...nothing.

The Time Is Now to move away from wanting to post our accomplishments for the sake of seeking praise or recognition. This only locks us in golden handcuffs. Instead, we can transition into posting for the sake of posting, without any need to fulfill our evolutionary needs—which interestingly enough, ends up satisfying them.

Pause and Ponder: Chapter Four

• How has my evolutionary blueprint influenced my career decisions?

• How does social media influence my perception of success and my own self-worth?

• In what ways can I prioritize my own happiness and well-being over the pursuit of external markers of success?

• How can I cultivate a greater sense of self-awareness and resist the pressures of the status game?

PART II

INTEGRATION

People are looking for ways of living whereby they don't live this fragmented, abstract, work-life that is completely cut off from all the rest of their truly human associations.

And so, we are facing a very big revolution in which our young people want to return to reality.

And even though what they do may make very little money, it will at least have the satisfaction of being an actual relationship to the real world in which we live now.

I don't know the detailed answers to all that, but this is what is coming. It will be very disruptive to things as we know them, but better by far.

Better by far to live in contact with the actual here-and-now than to live a life of perpetual suspense, waiting for a gorgeous thing that's going to turn up—but never, never does.

— *ALAN WATTS*

5

THE ALCHEMY OF GUT FEELINGS

Have the courage to follow your heart and intuition. They somehow already know what you truly want to become. Everything else is secondary.

— STEVE JOBS

We all have a sense of how impactful intuition is in our lives— often described as a "gut feeling" or a "sixth sense"—and it is perhaps the most underrated asset we possess for making decisions aligned with who we truly are. Many people attribute their best decisions to following their "gut feelings," sometimes to the point of saving lives. A vast amount of research reveals the power of intuition, especially when facing enormous challenges that are often riddled with uncertainty and complexity.

Gary Klein, a cognitive psychologist, has spent his career studying how we make decisions in complex and uncertain environments. Klein revolutionized the idea of naturalistic decision-making, which states that people often make decisions in situations where they do not have all the information they need, and can't spare the time to consider various options. In these situations, individuals must rely on their intuition and experience to make decisions quickly and effectively.[1] Klein's research has made such an impact in the world that even the White House Situation Room was redesigned based on his findings.[2]

His research shows that firefighters were more accurate in their judgments about the location of a fire when they relied on their intuition than when they deliberated about the information.[3] Another interesting finding was that people were more likely to make accurate judgments about the trustworthiness of others when they relied on their intuition than through simple contemplation.[4]

Isn't the case that our daily lives are the definition of uncertainty and imperfect information? That's why nurturing our intuitive senses could yield great dividends for all of us.

When we think about decision-making, we often believe it is a function of how much thought we have put into a given situation. One such example is the stock market: Most people believe that making good trades is a function of one's reasoning skills, but a group of researchers decided to test this claim and see if "gut feelings" could actually yield better results. They recruited eighteen traders who engage in high-frequency trading—holding positions for seconds, minutes, or hours at the most—to determine whether those who tap into physical sensory signals could make more money.[5]

According to Annie Murphy Paul, previous guest on my podcast[6] and author of *The Extended Mind*, the ability to identify physical sensations that emerge from within us is better known as "interoception," which includes the capacity to sense pain, hunger, and even heart rate variability. These sensations tend to emerge whenever we must make crucial decisions.[7]

The stock market researchers discovered that those more "in tune" with their bodily sensations had better investment decisions. Even crazier, those who were able to sense their heartbeats had better profit-and-loss profiles and had survived more time in the market.[8]

Another great example, illustrated by a study conducted by neuroscientist Anthony Damasio and discussed by Annie during our interview as well as in her book, sheds light on how our bodies *know* before we do.

In an online card game experiment, participants were asked to turn over cards from one of four decks, each containing a reward or a punishment. Two decks contained more rewards than punishments, while the other two contained more punishments than rewards. Although participants were unaware of this pattern, their bodies reacted to the presence of a threat when they considered taking cards from the bad decks. Skin conductance, a measure of nervous system arousal, increased as the game progressed, indicating a physiological response to the stimuli. The most fascinating aspect of this experiment was that participants gradually learned to avoid the bad decks, despite their cognitive unawareness of the pattern.[9]

What does this mean for all of us? Our bodies are a storage of infinite knowledge. We tend to believe that the mind is the only piece of hardware we possess to process information. However, our entire intuitive system has been built to engage with the world in ways that our rational mind alone cannot. Yet, our modern belief system prioritizes thoughts over feelings. We could make the case that French philosopher, René Descartes (1596-1650), who coined the famous phrase *Cogito, ergo sum* ("I think, therefore I am") defined the way we engage with the reality around us: to exist means to *think*, not to *feel*.

Perhaps this is why we often regard emotions as useless and deceitful impressions. But the groundbreaking research on the human body's ability to learn and respond to stimuli sheds new light on how our internal sensations and bodily experiences can provide invaluable information—and how those who are more in tune with their internal sensations can harness this wisdom to enhance their understanding of their authentic selves and decision-making abilities.

It sounds simple, but most of our intuitions—and interoceptive abilities—are neglected and muted in today's world. The modern world seems designed to cut the cord between our intuition and ourselves since we are constantly bombarded with artificial stimuli. We're glued to a phone all day, perhaps doom-scrolling or being bombarded by the news of the day (firing up our amygdala and defense mechanisms), never present with others or ourselves, and are always in a rush to get to work or an appointment. Therefore, we never create a space to allow our intuition to emerge—and take charge!

Fortunately, we have ways we can tap into the power of our intuition.

To have a stronger connection with our interoceptive abilities, Annie suggests that when making a big choice, journaling our physical sensations and reviewing them after making the decision can help us "fine tune" our intuition. When we journal on how our body feels at the time and after contemplating a decision, we create a bridge between our gut feelings and our rational minds so they can begin working together.[10]

For example, how does your body feel when you are contemplating a leap of faith, or accepting a new job offer? How does your body feel when facing a choice between two alternative paths?

Another great tool to align with our interoception is meditation. Annie provides a great technique for meditation called a "body scan." When we meditate, we can check in with our physical sensations by scanning our body and seeing how it feels to power the connection between us and our bodies. This meditation doesn't take more than five minutes per day: just close your eyes, set the intention of connecting with your intuition and your body, and envision a golden ring that scans your body, starting from your feet and going all the way up to your crown.[11]

By meditating, or at least periodically checking in with how we feel, we can align with our true, infinite knowledge base.

Think about it for a second: you are a line of genes in the making for millennia! You have made it up until now with all the evolutionary heritage that comes with such a journey.

Your body is not dumb, you just have to be better in commanding your space suit!

In modernity, most life decisions we make often fall under the optimization umbrella—the famous cost-benefit analysis. When we think about the career we want to choose, we tend to analyze how much it will pay in the future in terms of networking, prestige, and actual earnings. We tend to neglect how these decisions make us *feel*. We become so caught up in the moment, so distracted by the constant bombardment of stimuli, that we never ask ourselves, "How does this decision feel?" Further, we have not built the all-important bridge between our feelings and thoughts. Instead, we tend to see them as rivals rather than allies.

When our families ask us, 'Why did you make that decision?' they expect us to have a detailed, rational play-by-play breakdown of why we acted as we did. And this answer is the one we validate. If we would answer with, "It just felt right" or "It felt wrong," they might perceive us as impulsive and irrational.

Our best compasses are our bodies and intuition. When we say, "that course of action just didn't bode well for me," and we have harnessed the power of our bodies to guide our decisions, we unlock an entirely new storage of infinite ancestral knowledge, which acts faster than reason ever could. That awareness has existed within us for far longer than our prefrontal cortex.

While this may seem like a rant against rationality, it is quite the opposite. Our rational minds evolved on top of our evolutionary instincts. So, why not create an alliance between them rather than live through a constant battle between them? What if our feelings powered our thoughts? What if we could move across the world, making quicker decisions based on a refined gut feeling without the need for an optimized explanation?

What if we allowed space for what was possible based in our intuitions instead of what was optimal?

The evidence is right there: intuition can lead us to great results when we face uncertainty and complexity without access to perfect information.

Isn't this the game of life?

When have we ever had *perfect* information?

When have we ever found ourselves in a situation with a definitive, certain, optimal outcome? The only certainty we have in life is that life is all about uncertainty. Intuitive action may be paradoxically the most *optimal* way we can clear the path forward.

Optimization and mechanization of life can then be seen with a new lens, both serving as safety blankets to make us feel protected and more certain about our decisions because the payoffs "seem" tangible. But the quicker we acknowledge the nature of the game —the uncertainty of it all—the more fulfilled we will become, as that realization is based on truth and obliterates the deceitful nature of our mechanical lives.

Imperfection is perfection in and of itself.

Perfection is an imperfection in and of itself.

Intuitive Action: The Only Path Forward

It's not always easy to follow the subtle energetic information the universe broadcasts, especially when your friends, family, coworkers, or those with a business interest in your creativity are offering seemingly rational advice that challenges your intuitive knowing.

To the best of my ability, I've followed my intuition to make career turns, and been recommended against doing so every time.

It helps to realize that it's better to follow the universe than those around you.

— *RICK RUBIN*

At one or many points during our lives, we all have felt as if we received a signal from above—as if *something* or *someone* is sending us a clue as we navigate our lives. I believe that the bridge between us and this seemingly magical realm is called intuition. Our intuitive instincts are deeply interconnected to everything around us, even if we can't perceive that at first glance on a conscious level (or, I should say, *especially* when we can't perceive that on a conscious level). We are always connected.

In today's world, being able to access this magical realm is one of the most neglected gifts we hold within ourselves—and probably the most important of them all.

Modernity has put a premium on rationalization and mechanization processes. The modern path has been carved out on a linear trajectory for all of us that puts a high price on crossing life "milestones," which tend to begin after graduating from high school. These events are a one-size-fits-all prototype for all Earth's humans: Get a degree, find a job, get a promotion, get married, have kids, and die. This straight line essentially negates the power of magic to manifest itself in our lives.

Linearity offers structure and stability, while intuition unveils wonder and possibility. Linearity provides a comforting rhythm to our days, while intuition brings magic to them.

By setting us up for a linear path, modernity works as a revolving door for humanity, allowing every individual to get a taste of life, enough to feel as if we live but never actually savor life through our authenticity and its magic. In other words, everyone gets a taste of each "milestone" experience, such as graduating, passing through adulthood, gaining recognition and praise, getting married and raising children, and retiring into the sunset.

The danger lies in treating these milestones as mere transitions, like revolving doors, rather than embracing the magic that each moment holds. Our lives, your life, all lives are filled with potential for enchantment.

It's a matter of opening our eyes to the magic that surrounds us.

With all these milestones, the only certainty is that the finish line keeps moving further away. We go through the motions, chasing after goals without finding a truly meaningful purpose, and often neglecting time with our loved ones. It's as if the sacrifices we make—missing out on moments with family and friends—are somehow justified by the promise of reaching that elusive "success."

Herbert Marcuse, a German Philosopher and Sociologist (1898-1979), wrote in *One-Dimensional Man: Studies in the Ideology of Advanced Industrial Society,* that modern societies have gotten to a stage where individuals build a false sense of happiness and empty satisfaction through consumerism and distraction.[12] He pointed out that we are working so many hours trying to earn money to fulfill our desires, that we no longer have the energy to critically question our lives, let alone criticize our social structures. Why would we? I don't blame us. Some spend over forty hours per week in a job they might not like and that act takes double the effort because they must keep up appearances—with façades—while actually working, and society expects us to come home and plot a social upheaval!

Marcuse believed that our systems are built ingeniously so that all incentives lead us to choose conformity over critical thinking, magic, and intuition. We choose the status quo over dissent because dissent takes you out of the game.[13]

We've gradually bought into this system, largely driven by the appeal of consumerism. Our free time is filled with distractions, a never-ending stream of entertainment to occupy us until the end. When we're not working, we're indulging in a 24/7 feast of cable channels, endless movies, late-night outings, and the occasional two-week vacation. The issue lies in the underlying belief that these distractions somehow make the time spent working worthwhile.

We've been conditioned to see work and life as separate, with one merely serving to support the other, rather than integrating them into a balanced, fulfilling whole.

The irony is that these supposed "breaks" from work fail to serve as opportunities for introspection and connection with our authentic selves—with our intuition. Instead, we seek refuge in distractions, filling our leisure hours with a relentless pursuit of amusement. We've become so accustomed to this cycle of work and distraction that we've lost sight of the true essence of life. The magic that lies in the present moment, the beauty of genuine connection, and the profound joy of self-discovery—these treasures are obscured by the constant buzz of manufactured entertainment.

Our collective is experiencing an energy crisis from playing fabricated games for which we didn't even sign up. What's more, the depletion of energy disconnects us from the universe and its magic.

In one of my previous jobs, I had to engage in a simple, straightforward task. The caveat: I had to accomplish this during off-work hours first thing in the morning. As you might imagine (now that you're deep into this book), I am not a fan of senseless instructions and people mingling with what I can and cannot do during my own hours. Even writing the last sentence made me cringe at how deranged that sounds: we have our own hours, and then we have work hours. Immediately, I said, "No."

I asked my boss if I could do this task once I arrived at the office instead of doing it first thing in the morning, and the answer was a straight no.

"We decide when you do this task, not you."

I realized the task was more related to control rather than actual, meaningful work.

What really did it for me was the underlying message: I didn't own my time; they did.

Now I realize that time is too precious to keep saying "yes" to orders given that directly compromise a part of who I am and want to be in this world.

Mundane work that we embark on, however small, disconnect us from meaningful, magical, and masterful work—creative work! The more time I spent doing tasks to please my bosses while neglecting my intuition, the less tethered I was to the magical realm of creativity.

The battle between my manufactured self and my true self had reached a truce. Luckily for me, my true self won. I acted upon what felt right, not what *seemed* right. I stayed true to myself, to my sense of integrity, not to what would provide a better future payoff—for the sake of "careerism."

My manufactured self had the upper hand for many years and took me to amazing places. I'm extremely grateful for those opportunities. But along the way, my heart was nearly lost, and my intuitive radar kept roaring for my attention.

Intuition is our strongest radar to connect with the signals the cosmos throws at us, leading us to our most authentic self. We have neglected this source for so long—through consumerism, obsessive work hours, meaningless tasks, and endless access to entertainment and distractions that have made us forget our unlimited source of magic, energy, and creativity. Let's start prioritizing and listening but most importantly, acting upon our intuition—the inner wellspring of our universal knowledge and truth.

Pause and Ponder: Chapter Five

- How does intuition currently influence my decision-making

process, and what steps can I take to cultivate a stronger connection with my inner voice?

• When do I notice my gut feelings becoming more prominent? How can I create more space for them to emerge, and how might my decisions change if I aligned with them more closely?

• After finishing my regular work, do I feel creatively energized to pursue what truly excites me? What actions can I take to nurture that creative spark?

6

STOP POLISHING A FALSE DIAMOND

Did you ever have a job that you hated and worked real hard at?

A long, hard day of work. Finally, you get to go home, get in bed, close your eyes, and immediately you wake up and realize...that the whole day at work had been a dream.

It's bad enough that you sell your waking life for minimum wage, but now they get your dreams for free.

— GUY FORSYTH

Life resembles a project we build upon and try to finish in some meaningful way. It's like a big block of marble we need to sculpt into something perfect.

We all strive to develop ourselves and become a better version of who we are in the present moment—trying to improve is a natural part of being human. What really matters is, for whom are we trying to improve? Is our driving force trying to be better for us, or for other people? To impress our father? To gain the approval of our social circle? To make our family proud? Are we trying to check a rationally derived box that society has implicitly commanded us to?

We must understand our intentions, our driving force, so our intentionality is properly aligned.

It took me a while to come to terms with this realization—that the sculpture I was building for a long time was really for others to appreciate, and never for me to savor. But I am glad I came to this realization during my early twenties, as when we become older, our minds become too rigid (up to a neurological level) to do something other than reminisce about what could have been if we had followed our heart. Literally, as we age, our brains undergo structural changes that affect cognitive functions. Research indicates that neuroplasticity—the brain's ability to form and reorganize synaptic connections—declines over time, making it difficult for older adults to embrace new experiences or consider alternative life paths.[1]

Our life should, indeed, be treated as a big block of marble that needs sculpting. But the secret to a perfect sculpture is one you are not really trying to develop by brute, mechanical and systematic force. It's about allowing your colors guide your hand until the moment the sculpture is finished without you even knowing it. But there's a catch: There's not just one big block of marble. There are plenty.

Why do we box our life into a one-dimensional journey? Why can't we allow life's chapters to develop by themselves and learn when they are over or just starting? Why do some of us willingly work for forty years in the same company, while hating every second of it?

Many people who choose this path suffer from the sunk-cost bias.

In its simplest form, the sunk-cost bias suggests that we tend to stick with familiar routines, with activities we have done for a long time, because we have "sunk" too much effort, time, money into them, making backing out seem impossible—perhaps even shameful.[2]

This is especially evident in gambling: we keep placing bets because it's what we've been doing even if we are already at a loss and because we've already invested too much money, falsely believing that maybe, just maybe, right under our next bet the jackpot is hiding. However, more often than not, we're not one bet away from winning. In reality, we're already losing way past what we expected we would (perhaps a perfect metaphor for a life driven by careerism).

Many investors too face the sunk-cost bias: "I have invested too much money in this strategy. So, I can't backtrack now." In our careers, we can also fall victims to the sunk-cost bias: "I went to college to attain a finance degree, and I took student loans to finance my education. I have worked in the same industry for years, rising within the corporate ranks, and quitting seems impractical, as it signals that all my efforts have gone to waste."

If you ever heard someone say, "I have been working at this company for many years, and if I quit now, that would mean that all these years have been a complete waste of time. Therefore, I must continue my journey to become a partner in my firm even though I hate every waking minute I spend working with these toxic people," they are probably holding tight onto a dream turned into a nightmare due to the sunk-cost bias.

Throughout life we get X degree, X job, we meet X person, and we invest our time doing these things constantly for a while—even at the expense of our own well-being, just because we have spent too much time within these activities. Instead of trying something else, something new, we obsess trying to polish a diamond that perhaps was not meant to be polished.

Approaching life this way is like trying to fit a square peg into a round hole. Pointless, and doomed to fail.

While quitting might seem very costly, the true cost occurs when we don't follow our intuition in how we should allocate our time on Earth. Sure, quitting has a cost, but these consequences become smoother over time. In the present moment, when the decision is made, it might feel like a shock that we won't be able to pass through, but that is a fallacy. The only thing impossible to overcome is the failure to try.

Quitting your job could put your finances at risk and prevent you from seeing what opportunities might lie ahead. However, consider whether staying is worth it if it means losing touch with yourself, your values, and your passions; moving on from that toxic relationship may seem crazy after all those years together, but consider the cost of staying *just for the sake of staying*.

I believe it's not worth it. The cost is too high.

I believe we are put on this Earth to do far more than go through the motions or be a victim of the sunk-cost bias.

I believe that thinking about the cosmic significance of our lives deepens our perspective and reverence for our time on Earth— and, correspondingly, others' life journeys. It also reduces the chances of falling into a path driven by the sunk-cost bias.

While we have been told that saving money for forty years is a pathway to freedom (again, not to demonize money or wealth), that doesn't mean we must continue to give aspects of ourselves away to chase society's perception of success for decades, just to recover the freedom we once enjoyed as children.

This does not mean that we should always quit when the going gets tough. It's about choosing *your* tough.

Removing the chains of the sunk-cost bias for once and taking that leap of faith in your career might not bring immediate results, and the fruits of your efforts may take years to manifest. But that doesn't mean the journey itself should be filled with struggle. Those confined to cubicles, dictated by dress codes and corporate thinking, might find themselves in a system where productivity smothers creativity. Busyness becomes the norm, but the rewards of this path are hollow, failing to nourish their deeper desires.

The truth is, we are far wealthier than we realize—our wealth lies in the time we still have ahead of us. Refusing to slip into the golden handcuffs that shackle so many is a daunting task, but a necessary one. I believe we are collectively beginning to wake up. We are starting to realize that life holds more value than society's script has led us to believe, and we are beginning to reclaim the narrative. We are refusing to trade our time for hollow rewards, and instead, we're choosing the richness of a life aligned with purpose. We are waking up to the fact that our time is worth more than any digit in our bank account.

We are realizing that wealth tends to follow the soul, but the soul does not necessarily chase wealth. We are waking up to the fact that dollar signs follow the soul, but the soul does not necessarily follow the dollar signs.

Our present way of valuing a great life is through the most tangible one—our bank accounts. An easy way of quantifying our existence and rationalizing our success, but it is not an accurate way of weighing our time on Earth. It doesn't come close.

Imagine taking a pause from the relentless pursuit of external validation and the ceaseless quest for the next big thing. Imagine carving out a space for introspection, for daring to ask yourself the very questions you've been avoiding: Who am I, truly? What do I yearn for, deep within the core of my being? What sparks my soul, igniting a flame of passion that burns brighter than any fleeting distraction?

Don't let the sunk-cost fallacy hold you back from your true journey. Just because you've poured time and effort into your job, career, project, relationship or a marble sculpture doesn't mean it's destined for an external definition of completion.

Sometimes, the most powerful act of creation is knowing when to say "enough."

It's your piece of art, your own unique expression in this world. Don't be afraid to let go of perfection and embrace the beauty of imperfection. It might just be the finishing touch that transforms your work into a masterpiece.

Don't be afraid to let go when your instincts tell you it's time. Embrace the freedom to explore new avenues, to discover new passions, new loves, and to create art that is authentically yours. The world awaits your unique vision, your willingness to challenge the status quo and embrace the magic of the unfinished.

The beautiful aspect of our lives is that it's ever-changing, dynamic, emergent, and intriguing. The search is the end goal. The sculpture will ultimately emerge in its final form, but the end goal is not about finishing. Instead, it's about discovering what's inside that big block of monolithic marble.

Be Careful What You Sacrifice

If you are willing to do it at all costs, it will likely cost you everything. If you do whatever it takes, likely it'll take everything. That tells you everything you need to know.

— *PAUL PORTESI*

The Aztecs believed sacrifices could appease gods and ensure good fortune and protection. They felt strongly that human sacrifice would create and maintain balance in the universe, put a stop to droughts, or prevent disasters. The Egyptians also believed that sacrifice was a way to receive blessings from the gods.

Sacrifice used to be a way for us to show gratitude or devotion to a significant force outside us, such as God. Rituals offering our crops, our goods, our animals, and sometimes even our own people were some of the ways we showed our respect for cosmic forces.

Fortunately, we no longer believe we need to sacrifice humans to "guarantee" universal balance. We do, however, still believe in the power of sacrifice as a prerequisite for greatness.

Some of the greatest athletes cite sacrifice as an essential factor in their success, like Tiger Woods, widely considered one of the greatest golfers of all time. He enjoyed a record-breaking career and is arguably one of the most important sports icons in history. His story reflects the true cost of success and the deceptive nature of sacrifice in modern history. He truly embodies the saying, "They see the glory but don't know the whole story." For most of us who desire greatness in our lives, we want glory but don't want to hear the real story.

Chris Williamson, host of the Modern Wisdom Podcast and previous guest on my podcast[3], described the concept of wanting to be great without paying the price of greatness:

> "...You look at somebody that has ostensibly had it all sorted out, Elon Musk as an example, or Tiger Woods. You look at these guys and think, 'I'd love to have Elon Musk's work ethic or his IQ or whatever, or I'd love to have Tiger Woods' golfing ability.' Hang on a second; you don't get to pick little items from that person's wardrobe and put them on like you're in a store. It's a onesie; this isn't pick-and-choose; this isn't a wholesale sale..."[4]

In other words, we often see what we want to see but fail to realize how much it takes to get to such a high altitude of the 'greatness mountain.'

It will likely cost you everything if you're willing to do it at all costs.

From a very young age, Tiger endured a rigorous training regimen and strict discipline, which required him to sacrifice a typical childhood, leisure time, and many normal social interactions. This intense focus on golf allowed him to excel in the sport but meant missing out on many aspects of a balanced upbringing.

If you believe that winning is all that matters in life, by all means, take the deal Tiger took. But understand that the cost might be not having an integrated sense of self, little to no self-worth, and the inability to maintain a relationship.

Is that a price you are willing to pay?

The crazy part is that we never realize the true price of greatness, which is that it might cost us everything. Setting ambitious objectives can be one of the most deceitful decisions we can make.

Chasing greatness, in the conventional sense, like becoming the best golfer of all time, can be more costly in the long run than just choosing to play golf for the love of it and see what emerges from it.

When we become overly attached to reaching a goal, such as becoming the greatest of all time in any field, the underlying costs of the chosen path come at a high price. Play no longer feels like play. At that point, we should begin to redefine what the concept of sacrifice should entail.

While ancient sacrifices were made for higher purposes, such as appeasing the gods, modern sacrifices are often reduced to a cost-benefit analysis that simplifies our path. This approach can leave us feeling empty inside. Worse still, we often deceive ourselves into believing that any goal we sacrifice for is inherently worth the sacrifice.

One thing is certain: the pursuit of our treasure requires sacrifices. However, we often sacrifice our own well-being and happiness, treating them transactionally while chasing elusive and predatory notions of "success." This approach leads us to pursue intangible, yet seductive ideas that may not truly fulfill us.

The equation has reversed itself in such a way that the true benefit of the sacrifice, which is intended to make us feel better, is strangling our inner selves.

For many people, the sacrifice has become this: putting their creative passions and happiness on hold while chasing money, prestige, and success, with the intention of pursuing their true passions later. In doing so, we sacrifice the preciousness of our time in exchange for external rewards that often leave us feeling empty. Sacrifices should work the other way around: they should enhance our lives now, with the hope of future betterment. If we're already sacrificing our time today for a better tomorrow, we should at least try to pursue something that fulfills us along the way.

While we latch on to the almost cosmic truth that sacrifice precedes success, we must realize that sacrifice, in itself, should take place around what we love to do.

Only then will we receive the real blessings from the gods—when we sacrifice for what we love, rather than sacrificing what we love for a false idea.

Intentionally Failing

> Ever tried. Ever failed. No matter. Try Again. Fail again. Fail better.
>
> — SAMUEL BECKETT

Let's be clear about one thing: there are no limits to what you can accomplish. And I believe the biggest accomplishment we can make is to fail—to fail often...to fail with intention.

What if we set ourselves up for failure, and that, in itself, is setting us up for success? By intentionally failing, I mean exposing ourselves to the most ambitious aspirations we have where the most likely outcome is us failing. If you set yourself with the core goal of failing that, in and of itself, means becoming a great success.

It sounds stupid and highly counterintuitive, but if our goal is to fail and we succeed in failing, we are therefore successful people.

Collectively, we have put a premium on maximizing success, so much so, that we shy away from pursuing the real exciting activities we like because they seem unlikely to realize into existence.

Let me be very clear: nothing was ever promised to you. You were never meant to be "something" or become "someone." Like Frank Underwood, a fictitious character of the TV show *House of Cards*, said, "You are entitled to nothing." This may sound harsh, but it is extremely liberating once you fully digest the concept—up to the point where you might actually become someone. Allow me to illustrate it with a personal story:

One of my core passions is playing baseball. When I am on-field training and fielding some ground balls, it almost feels as if I am meditating. My mind, gradually as I grew up, transformed my love for baseball into a single thought: "Baseball has to be my destiny. It is the only path for me to be happy." Then, a whole lifestyle began to be shaped around baseball. I would train, then go to school, then train more. As I made progress, the thought became, "If I don't become a baseball player, I'll be forever unhappy." Now that's the kind of pressure that transforms dreams into nightmares; the mechanical mind kicks in, the guilt emerges, and what once felt like meditation transforms into a senseless obsession.

See, the problem with believing there is a destiny you need to fulfill is that your rational mind kicks in and what once was a joy for you—like playing baseball—becomes a full-time job, with metrics and objectives and quotas and expectations where the stakes suddenly become high, so unattainable, that your life's destiny is on the line.

Play stops being playful and it becomes dreadful.

My intention with baseball was pure enjoyment, and then it got butchered, by myself, as I tried to fit into the identity of a baseball player. As I labeled this passion with all these superfluous expectations and seriousness.

Once the rational mind gets hold of your desire, it will do whatever it can to transform it into a metric, into something measurable that needs to gradually show progress—we transform a dream into a benchmark in our bottom line.

That's how modernity works: we are all obsessed with trying to pass milestones, with quantifying existence, and measuring ourselves with the word *progress*.

Well, speak to anyone who has retired and ask them if checking boxes from their to-do lists gave them lasting satisfaction.

Ask them if their destiny would have been fatally different without checking the boxes of success. Almost all will answer the same way, "I was so caught up in trying to achieve that I forgot what truly mattered in life, which boils down to faith, family, friends, and fulfillment." Any of our wise elders will tell you how little it matters if you become a CEO or create a trillion-dollar company at the cost of your true self.

We all have a clock counting down toward the end of our time on Earth. We can't escape it. I used to think that the best way to enjoy life was through accomplishments and building an identity based on pure success and gold stars. Now I subscribe to experimenting with my colors, being led by what moves me, and seeing where that takes me—which until this point has been only successful experiences on my own terms.

In modernity we have been told that life is linear, and we must follow a recipe to become successful. "It takes a long time to build something," some say, implying we must stay true to our craft if we wish to reap fruit from it.

I wholeheartedly agree with this. Good things take time, but what if your true craft was never within sight, because you took this advice at the moment you became a financial advisor, and you totally hated every single minute of it (since good things take the time), and you decided to stick it out for sixty years, and nothing ever happened (recall the sunk-cost bias discussed earlier). What if, instead of approaching life as a project, you embrace life as a journey?

What if I told you that you didn't need to accomplish anything and that life was supposed to be led by life itself, led by your inner self? What if I told you that you haven't really immersed yourself within your true self, trusted life to guide you, let alone introduced yourself to this idea because modernity told you to stick to the script and linearize your life as much as possible?

What if i told you the fact that you are alive right now means you have won the game of life?

I was never meant to be just a baseball player, a politician, or a writer—or confined to any other single identity. I've come to realize that life is too short to limit myself to these labels. There is nothing to be fulfilled except the pursuit of fulfillment itself. The identities we adopt will naturally emerge as byproducts of following our life force.

True fulfillment comes from experimenting your humanity and allowing it to forge your unique path. It's about riding a wave until the wave fades out and then riding another wave. Life is not about seeing how much your net worth can become—it's too short, too precious for that.

Chasing fame, money, and success does not do your life justice. If you're like me (which is extremely likely since you have read this book up until now), you have so many creative interests it is an injustice to your time and others' for you not to explore them.

Why obsess over trying to wear the hat of a baseball player, politician, singer, or comedian for an entire lifetime? Why not try out all things without the need to accomplish anything? Trying out and perhaps failing is the accomplishment.

Back to my baseball story. One day, I went to a walk-on tryout at my alma mater when I was a senior, and I was sure I would be recruited—until I saw the 6'5," 200-pound players trying out. My first reaction was...I should bail. I'll never make the team. But then, the eureka moment arrived: "I won't make the team. There's absolutely no way. I have failed even without trying. But, you know what? I'll make the most out of the experience." So, I pitched, played infield, played outfield, and hit some line drives while others were serious about their chances even though they didn't have any. I even asked for a bullpen session after I watched a gigantic 17-year old throw at ninety miles per hour. I laughed at his speed, told the pitching coach to get ready and make sure to take out his radar gun to see actual out-of-this-world velocity.

I clocked in at seventy miles per hour at my maximum speed.

The coaches laughed, and so did I. I told them, "You'll sign me if I hit seventy-one miles per hour on this one." They took the deal to continue with the fun. With all my might, strength, and soul...I pitched at sixty-nine miles per hour. More laughter broke loose. We had a great time.

I even celebrated when my "competition," those trying to get a place on the roster, made a great play. Most of the kids trying out stared at me like I was crazy. "Why would you cheer for the guy who will take your place?" they asked. The answer was, because I had already arrived. There was no need to do anything else. I didn't need the roster spot, and I didn't need to fulfill my destiny as a baseball player. I had arrived.

For me, this was all that I required. Of course if the spot had been offered I would have accepted it. But the point is that I slowly began to dissociate fulfillment from outcome—fulfillment emerged from experience rather than the metrics.

For many, the thought of failing to hit a metric, a milestone, is so daunting they remove themselves from the equation because a non-attempt is not registered in the record book, whereas a failed attempt is.

The real failure comes when you don't allow yourself to fail. Suppose your goal is to fail, and you are successful at it and fail constantly. In that case, you are the most successful person that has ever lived while paradoxically increasing the odds of actually succeeding in terms of metrics. This manifests as a byproduct, not as the main purpose.

In the grand scheme of things, taking into account the Big Bang, the fact that there have been billions of humans living before you and who will live after you, that Planet Earth has existed for trillions of years before you and it will continue to do so after you, that we are more than eight billion evolved chimpanzees living who—hopefully—brush their teeth at least in the morning and at night, and are obsessed with metrics, what *is* failure, anyway?!

It's a pure illusion instilled in us that has killed more dreams than any other virus.

And what is success, anyway?

Success means you have found—or are looking for—that which you love doing, or have at least realized you don't know what that is, and are willing to embark on your path to discovering it, and failing intentionally along the way.

Pause and Ponder: Chapter Six

• Who am I, truly?

• What do I yearn for, deep within the core of my being?

• What sparks my soul, igniting a flame of passion that outshines any fleeting distraction?

• How does the idea of striving for perfection resonate with me?

• What am I afraid might happen if I 'fail'?

• Where in my life could I fail miserably and still consider it a massive success?

• What tradeoffs am I willing and unwilling to make to reach my goals?

• Am I continuing to work towards something in my life only because I've 'sunk' time into it?

7

SLAY THE SERPENT

"The spirit of evil is fear, negation, the adversary who opposes life in its struggle for eternal duration and thwarts every great deed, who infuses into the body the poison of weakness and age through the treacherous bite of the serpent; he is the spirit of regression, who threatens us with bondage to the mother and with dissolution and extinction in the unconscious.

For the hero, fear is a challenge and a task, because only boldness can deliver from fear. And if the risk is not taken, the meaning of life is somehow violated, and the whole future is condemned to hopeless staleness, to a drab grey lit only by will-o'-the-wisps."

— C.G. JUNG

The modern workplace is a place where creativity goes to die. It's a mind virus with multiple faces like Hydra, the many-headed monster from Greek Mythology. According to the myth, each time it had one of its heads cut off, two more would grow in its place.

Hydra was invincible—that is, until the Greek Hero, Hercules, came onto the scene.

Just like Hydra, our misconception about how life needs to unfold—the idea built around the notion that life happens to us rather than us happening to life, that our lives have to be built around our careers rather than our careers based in our lives, can obliterate us single-handedly. However, each time someone tries to cut off the head of conformity—whether it's the relentless chase for wealth accumulation, status-seeking, or any other societal pressure—two new heads grow in its place. Each head represents another facet of the same monster: obsessive wealth accumulation, status-seeking, and wasting our time and creative nature. This monster has gained a strength unlike any other, and it controls us as its puppets.

Hydra has permeated our life in many ways, including self-doubt, submissiveness to outside influences, fear of the unknown, lost integrity, and other negative emotions that put a full stop to our true creative potential.

We must become our own Hercules. We too have the power to "Slay the Serpent," We too can overcome the seemingly impossible challenge of betting on ourselves and realizing that our potential can be unleashed like magic, but only if we resist conformity and embrace our creative potential.

It is crucial to slay the serpent, in part, because it would replace the toxic self-fulfilling cycle of greed, temptation, and conformity with one that works as a spiral of prosperity. When we slay our insecurities, discard false life scripts, and abandon our ego-driven pursuits, we can truly connect with our creative interests through intuition and passion. This process is about constructing a life that reflects our authentic selves—a life driven by what genuinely excites and fulfills us. By building our world from this genuine place, we inspire others with our authenticity, spreading our truest colors.

Thus, we energize ourselves through our creations: you are reading a book that emerged from my most authentic self, you just might become inspired to build something you love just for the sake of loving it. Then, someone else sees your craft and awakens to the sincerity of that decision and becomes inspired to add sincerity to their own craft, and so on.

This cycle of prosperity can often feel intangible, as the connections between each step may not always be immediately clear. However, just because we can't always see the evidence doesn't mean it isn't there. This unseen momentum often works quietly in the background, gradually shaping our growth and success.

Truth be told, many of us are under the influence of other "mind viruses" originating from a Hydra-like source. These mind viruses manifest as various ideologies that hijack our ability to think independently. For example, some people may adopt Socialism as their core identity, describing themselves on social media as "revolutionaries fighting class warfare." Meanwhile, others identify as Capitalists, proudly calling themselves "hardcore free enterprise supporters." We see similar identities with feminists, Marxists, atheists, religious followers, and anarchists. Many of us live under the spell of these "–ists," which shape us to fulfill their agendas. These identities often wear us, instead of us wearing them.

As Anu Atluru writes on X,

"people can tell when you're wearing something you don't love, and sometimes that thing you're wearing is an identity."[1]

Other extrinsic influences, like memes, also drive conformity. British evolutionary biologist Richard Dawkins conceived of memes as units of cultural transmission—ideas, behaviors, or styles that spread within a culture much like genes do in biology. These memes replicate, evolve, and adapt independently, living within our minds and shaping how we think, act, and connect with the world.[2] More often than not, negative memes are planted into our minds and stay there forever.

Most of us spend an entire life fighting to protect these memes, and that is because we don't possess ideologies, ideologies possess us. A cycle of toxicity, despair, and insecurity has captured many minds.

But we can fight back once we realize how we can use memes to our advantage. If we know that mind viruses exist, we can evaluate what kind of deceptive ideas are ruling our lives: Why have we accepted it as natural law that it's worth spending forty years of our lives paying for a mortgage, being enslaved by a job we hate? Why have we golden-cuffed our existence? Above all else, why have we considered ourselves as productive assets rather than a force of creativity?

Once we realize how strong a hold some of these ideas have on us, we can begin to replace them with new ideas, new questions that ignite the engines of the spiral of prosperity:

• How can I build a life around my creative nature?

• What kinds of activities do I love doing just for the sake of enjoyment?

• How can I positively infect others through those activities?

• What would the world look like if we all gained energy from our work rather than feeling drained by it?

If we all embrace our true creative powers, pursue the things we love, and act upon them for the sake of our love for them, we can infect others with positivity.

An obvious example of this is when someone cooks for us, such as our grandmothers. In my case, my Nona (who is of Greek Heritage and learned her mother's recipes) is one of the best cooks I know. And I always ask her: "Nona, what is your secret ingredient?" and she always replies: "I cook with love. When someone prepares a meal with love, you can taste it in your food. That's the secret."

Love is the ultimate force-multiplier, the antidote to conformity, and the secret to slaying Hydra. When we create from a place of love, we infuse our work with authenticity and purpose, breaking free from societal scripts that demand conformity. When my Nona prepares a meal with love, that love becomes tangible in the experience of eating it. This simple act carries forward, influencing me to act with the same intention and spreading a chain of positivity.

By creating with love—whether it's writing a book, crafting a piece of art, or simply preparing a meal—we align ourselves with our truest essence. This process not only liberates us from the hold of societal expectations but also inspires others to break free from their own constraints. Love becomes the foundation for building a world rooted in authenticity and connection.

Carl Jung, the Swiss psychoanalyst and psychologist, wrote in his book, *Memories, Dreams, Reflections*, that we tend to follow memes mindlessly, these social conventions and codes, because of a creeping fear of criticism and of being different from the herd:

"Deep down, below the surface of the average man's conscience, he hears a voice whispering, 'There is something not right,' no matter how much his rightness is supported by public opinion or by the moral code."[3]

Fearing criticism is entirely justifiable through our evolutionary blueprint: If we are part of a herd rather than an outcast, our odds of being killed by a predator decrease exponentially, and our odds of reproducing increase because we fit kindly into society. But conforming does nothing other than mute our inner voice below the surface of our conscience that tells us something's off—that inner whisper identifies how we are trying to build a life through deception and fear.

That voice never goes away.

It can become less potent throughout life, for sure, but it will always remain there and express itself in some way. For Jung, not following that inner voice could lead to psychological distress and even cause disintegration of the psyche, leading to neuroticism, anxiety, and psychological disorders, such as depression.

Following social norms rather than intuitive feelings manifests itself throughout our entire lives, and our systems are an external representation of this self-deceptive and destructive behavior.

Of course, we feel disconnected from others, we're literally disconnected from ourselves. Of course we live atomized lives, because we are not fully integrated within ourselves. Of course we feel a lack of purpose and meaninglessness in what we do throughout our entire adult life—it's because we don't inquire about what 'purpose' really means for us.

On the flip side, all of us hear that voice. If we engage actively with it through self-inquiry, there is an immense opportunity for our macro-life paradigms to radically change and reflect who we truly are. More often than not we fail to recognize that this way of living is a choice we all make, day in and day out. That provides a great opportunity for us to actively build the world we want to live in, one that aligns with who we truly are rather than just normalizing the idea that this voice is merely a byproduct of living a dull life.

When we embrace our authenticity, we cast a ripple effect into the world that infects and shows others that it is actually possible to live an extraordinary life that only we define, independently from extrinsic forces, without sacrificing the deepest, most sincere aspects of our nature.

That is how the spiral of prosperity begins. We confront challenges head on. We become self reliant. We find our own courage. We Slay the Serpent.

Are You a Dreamer, or a Sheep?

> A good person will follow the rules. A great person will follow himself.
>
> — *MARK SCOUT, SEVERANCE*

As we have covered throughout this book, somewhere along the way we removed ourselves from the life equation to join a lifeless, pale-looking herd for a big desk and a big paycheck. When we take a step back, we begin planting the seeds of redefining what a successful life means, and that starts by looking inward.

I must stress, careers do not need to be an enemy of fulfillment, but must not be confused with self-realization for the wrong reasons. Many can find genuine joy within a career path that aligns with their core selves. But it's seems that this is not the norm, as many Millennials and Get Z report having experienced depression[4] and more reports of less social life and bonding.[5]

What is all this talk about depths of despair? Why are so many people depressed, lost, and alone? Why do many people cite mental health reasons for quitting their jobs? Why are wages stagnant yet working hours continue to be more demanding?

Since 2013, there has been a forty-seven percent increase in major depression diagnoses for Millennials, by sixty-five percent among adolescent girls and by forty-seven percent among adolescent boys.[6] This is beyond awful—it is despicable and outrageous and should be considered a global emergency.

But instead, our proposed solutions are trying to "Advil it." That is, they are trying to numb the feelings of despair rather than getting to their root cause. Solutions like making the workplace an entertaining, Zen place that features meditation hubs tell us that something is off.

But there's a silver lining to all this: we can wake up to the realization that we are the key that unlocks everything else. When we realize we have a sense of agency in our life, regardless of the external turmoil that continues to grow daily, we take back the power. In a very literal sense, we become unstoppable.

The solutions to our challenges will never be handed to us. They can only emerge from within. True change only comes from realizing how special our time on Earth really is and how much we are wasting it trying to "quick fix" our way out of our problems. We won't solve the mental health crisis by adding meditation hubs into our workplace, we won't solve the student loan crisis by offering more amenities to our students, and we sure as hell won't solve the lack of meaning in our work by enhancing the "work-life balance" equation.

Through a sense of agency, resilience can be nurtured. Before we get to a world that is built around the spiral of prosperity, we first must be able to rip off the band aid and understand it will hurt. Think about it like a toxic relationship: you know you must break up, but you also know you're hooked on that feeling.

In the same way, we have become addicted and conditioned to believe this style of life is natural. But the numbers tell a completely different story. To nurture resilience, we must first be up to the challenge of turning inward, perhaps by taking a sabbatical and taking the illusory "risk" of following our intuition, regardless of how painful it might feel initially. Others may question every decision we make and the uncertainty of choosing ourselves. But we must allow the answers—our answers—to emerge from within, however "risky" our actions may appear to others.

We must awaken to the fact that we have already won the game. We are alive right now!

We have family, friends, and access to a community. Above all else, we woke up today. We get another chance to take the *illusory* risk of following our gut. We get another opportunity to pursue our creative passions; the fact that we are alive in this present moment means we have won the cosmic lottery. In that sense, everything else life throws at us, every single challenge, is a tailwind in our favor.

It's not too late to realize that the key we've been searching for has always been inside us. We are the key to finding our lock. The search is what makes the game of life worthwhile. It's about searching for treasure that only we can open.

If you are reading this book, deep within you, there's a feeling that the search may have not begun. Start now! Never let despair triumph. Build a world of positivity and optimism through your actions. Choose yourself first and, in that way, choose others.

———

You Are the Key

Invariably, people want to change you to fit with what they're doing. Real search isn't changing what's inside of you. It's allowing what's inside of you to emerge to find where you fit. Self-help books try to change you. You're the key to find your lock. It's the search.

— *PAUL PORTESI*

In our times, we have been conditioned to believe that we must fit into other people's agendas and plans. We have been sold the idea that if we play their game for a sufficiently long time, we'll be able to own that game.

Not true. Not true! We don't read the fine print that says we must change everything about us to receive that reward. And once the reward does come, we feel unrecognizable, almost as if we betrayed ourselves.

We haven't really given ourselves the time to allow what's inside of us to emerge. Our internal drives are muted due to social reasons and empty chases.

It's within the search that we reveal where we fit.

When we don't force ourselves to fit into other people's plans, we ultimately take control of who we are, and our colors can reveal themselves in accordance with our true nature.

So, it's less about fitting in and more about allowing our nature to emerge.

It's less about self-help books and more about listening to the self. Self-help books try to change us. They also sell a recipe to mold us into something we are not.

Allow self-help to emerge from your own soul. The special, uniquely subjective emotions that surface when you take a step back to reflect, project yourself authentically, and emerge into the light of the true self.

Taking a step back often means moving forward. Unfortunately for most, taking a step back is not a choice, either because they're afraid of starting from zero, or feel too immersed in the role they are playing. On a macro scale, it's clear these "robotic" decisions don't work out for most of us.

When uncomfortable emotions emerge, most of us shut them down to continue carving a path that probably was not meant for us.

But I ask you: What is a life without having explored these emotions? Is it worth repressing the unique facets of your humanity for the sake of a career? Does it pay to hide these emotions to keep up appearances?

Absolutely not.

Those who dive deep into their uncomfortable emotions emerge even stronger with a newly discovered integrated sense of self.

The truth is that life will never be filled with awards, accolades, praises, or external success. In fact, these seem to have the opposite effect on almost everyone who has accomplished incredible feats in exchange for their true self. They become lifeless, drained, and purely artificial. Life's real rewards come when you realize that you are the key that unlocks everything else.

For some crazy reason, we have forgotten this simple yet powerful idea: Only *we* can unlock everything else.

It is not the diploma, not the awards, not the praise. It is definitely not climbing the corporate ladder while suffering each waking moment, and it is certainly not by exchanging our humanity for a paycheck.

All the answers flow when we tap into our hearts and hear its authentic voice, but most of us are too afraid to listen to what the heart has to say.

In a way, these fears are legitimate. The heart speaks direct truths. It does not hold back, and we all know it. That is why we have silenced it as much as possible. The truth, however powerful, still hurts.

But this hurt is exactly the kind of hurt we need: truthful, raw, authentic hurt that leads to real, genuine growth.

Ironically, this kind of hurt is the most healing thing we can look for.

Allow that idea to sink in a bit more.

That kind of hurt is precisely what will heal all of us.

That thought moved me so much that I had to pause my writing to share it with my grandmother, and she was also moved. She told me,

> "Alex, you should write more about this and add something I have been thinking about for a while now. You should tell your readers that yourself only belongs to you,

and myself only belongs to me. And when we accept this idea, we can enjoy the true personalities of each other and, in a way, unlock our true selves and share them with everyone."

Thank you, Nona, for this powerful idea. You belong to yourself and no one else.

Pause and Ponder: Chapter Seven

• How can I build a life that aligns with my creative nature?

• What activities bring me joy simply for the sake of doing them?

• How can I inspire and positively influence others through my craft?

• What would my life look like if my work energized me rather than drained me?

• Do I feel a disconnect between who I am and what I do for work?

• How do I define my identity both inside and outside of work?

• What is the "hydra" I need to confront, and how can I overcome it?

8

INTEGRATING LIFE AND WORK

Step into the fear in order to step into a life.

— JAMES HOLLIS

"Every time you find yourself here, it's because you chose to come back," said Mark Scout to his coworker. In the hit series Severance, Mark works at Lumen Industries, where employees have chips implanted to surgically divide their work and personal lives. This erasure serves as an escape from painful emotions, allowing them to bury their grief, anger, or longing under layers of meaningless tasks and bureaucratic processes. Mark, grieving the loss of his wife, uses his job as a refuge, avoiding the discomfort of self-reflection and personal growth. At work, he mindlessly clicks away at a screen to "refine data," incentivized by shallow rewards and fearful of punishment, while on weekends, he numbs himself with junk food and isolation.

Like the characters in Severance, we often use work as a maze to distract ourselves from confronting the deeper, transformative emotions that could truly free us.

Our lives have become overly-reliant on maintaining this status quo, often sidelining the real, transformative work we need to do —the kind that is challenging, internal, and ultimately rewarding.

Haven't we all been victims of engaging in such behaviors? Haven't we all used work as an excuse to distract ourselves from the pain we feel, from the challenges we face, and to repress the sometimes agonizing realization that we are not going to live forever—but thinking we can always start living our true lives "tomorrow"? How many times have we started a sentence with "I can't do X because of work." How many times have we exhausted ourselves doing meaningless tasks just so we can hide behind our "hard work" and cop out from what truly matters to us?

While *Severance* portrays a rather extreme scenario of the work-life balance concept, it shares a disturbing truth about how we engage with work: it reveals to us our reliance on unfulfilling jobs as a barrier against confronting our deeper issues. These roles help us avoid facing our inner demons, challenging our existential questions, and fully realizing our creative potential. They effectively place a 'justified' ceiling on how far we can grow.

Modern work has enabled us to dupe ourselves about deep realizations in our lives: our time is limited, our loved ones will not live forever, and time is ticking for us to finally live the lives we want to be living. For many, these truths are too real to digest, but if we reflect on how these realizations bring us closer to reaching our true potential and making a true creative dent in the universe, we will completely forget about the concept of work-life balance.

The notion of work-life balance is deceitful. Much like the employees in Severance, who implant a chip to erase personal memories during work hours, we often use work as an escape to suppress the "bothering" thoughts that truly matter. This creates a split identity: one that knows only work, devoid of personal pain or pleasure, encapsulated within the confines of an office cubicle, and another left to bear the unprocessed emotions and challenges during non-work hours. But no mask or chip can curtail our inherent humanity—the feelings that make us tick.

If we were one with our career, and our careers were aligned with our lives, we wouldn't need a work-life balance. The fact that we have to disassociate these two facets of our lives rather than holistically speak about them should be all the evidence we need that we are living fragmented lives.

There is nothing to balance if you are aligned with your core, with your heart, and with your mission on Earth. Why would you need to put a veil between you and your work? They are both intrinsically part of you. There is no longer a need for repressing emotions because you have embraced your shadow, you have gone deep into your own self, and your work reflects the sincerest aspects of yourself.

When we complain about how work is crossing a line and starts to interfere with our personal lives, and we judge companies for their lack of respect for the work-life balance, we face an obvious, but painful realization: we will not find our creative passion there.

If you need work-life balance it should be the immediate indicator that your life's work has not yet been found.

We enter that workplace for reasons not aligned with honoring our time on Earth. We do it to make ends meet, or to polish our curriculum vitae to land a better job afterwards with better pay and prestige. We do it because we think we'll live forever, and there's always a tomorrow to start living.

Yet the golden-cuffs scheme of life is built with many booby traps: you can only get a great education if you are willing to drown yourself with student loans that you pay in an average of twenty years or more; you can only get a house if you sign a thirty-year mortgage with up to a seven percent rate; you can only hope you'll never get injured or need medical assistance because of how ridiculous healthcare fees are. These challenges and a sense of meaninglessness from our careers place a heavy burden on many of us.

Again, I don't judge anyone's personal situation, and minute by minute the world is making it more difficult to build meaningful paths that pay our bills and make us feel whole. But the hurdles, the obstacles, and the excuses will only continue to multiply and deepen if we don't act upon the realization that we won't be here on Earth forever, and our time, our most valuable asset, is being wasted in meaningless pursuits.

While these ideas might be overwhelming, the first step reclaiming our creative nature is the simplest, yet most intimidating task: listening to our hearts.

The main reason people have opted into this system of being walking zombies is because we feel too intimidated to confront our hearts and accept that we have silenced their true desires. We also feel too guilty by the fact that we know, *we know*, we have mistreated our time on Earth. We are absolutely aware of it. All of us.

While many seem as if they're doing perfectly fine working a corporate job that pays a hefty salary, some people realize five to ten years later how big the sacrifice was just to chase a paycheck.

If you don't believe me, go to any grocery store at 6:00 p.m. and try to pay close attention to the energy everyone is carrying within them: Is it playful? Is it loving? Is it optimistic? If you observe closely, you will see how most people are walking around with despair in their eyes and in autopilot mode...almost as if we were walking zombies living through a meaning crisis.[1]

We have forgotten that we are happening to life and not the other way around.

You might say, "Alex, you are really putting a tremendous emphasis on the work-life balance. Do you genuinely believe this is a fundamental problem? Don't you believe that the current political climate, the heated conversation about a potential world war, and the looming prospects of climate change have more to do with the despair that some of us feel?"

While these questions are entirely valid, I believe these problems arise from the same source: We are afraid to realize our time on Earth is limited, and we don't really grasp the fact that this automatically means other peoples' time is finite too.

George Gurdjieff, a spiritual teacher and philosopher who lived in the late nineteenth and early twentieth centuries, said that individuals should confront the reality of their own mortality to awaken to a deeper understanding of themselves and the world around them. He deeply believed that by doing so, it would be the one thing that could possibly save humankind from its 'idiocy'— namely, political division, hate, and selfishness.[2]

When we finally realize we are together on this blue marble, crossing a vast, deep, dark ocean as one big family, there is simply no room for negative feelings toward anyone. When this realization hits you intensely, there will not be any self-doubt that you should quit your nonsense job which you have continuously rationalized over time, and your crystal clear purpose will finally shine before you: your duty is not to separate your life from your work but to become one with your work, to work obsessively on your true calling, which can only emerge if you give yourself the space for it to truly emerge.

But believe me when I say that the calling will never arrive for those who continue down the path of severing life and work and allegedly 'balancing' two completely isolated layers of life.

Let us remember what Mark said: Every time we go back to work at a place we are not fully integrated with, not fully aligned with, it's a choice we, only we, make.

As creators, let us too remember that we can decide to stop the "work-life balance" nonsense, and be one with our creative nature.

Anti-Ambition or Genuine Ambition?

For older generations, Millennials and Gen Zs seek to have a "soft life," meaning that their life consists of less discomfort, less effort, more community related activities, and less career centrism—sort of the complete opposite of ambition. One article heavily criticized the idea of "soft life," because according to the writer, the term means that people stop sacrificing and choose a life solely consisting of pleasantries.[3] But is that not what everyone strives to enjoy after retirement?

The following anecdote illustrates this point: As a man walked in a field, he spotted another sitting under a tree, strumming a guitar, and lazing in the sun.

The man approached the other and inquired, "What are you doing?"

"I'm just sitting under this tree, singing, relaxing, and enjoying the sunshine," came the reply.

"How can you be so lazy? I have a sixteen-hour-a-day job—I work all the time. I'm never home, and I barely have time to spend with my family. It's a tremendous sacrifice, but it's worth it—I make a lot of money."

"And why do you do that?" the man said, looking up, delighting in the sun's warmth.

"That's a silly question. I work hard so I can retire and go on vacation with my family."

"What will you do on vacation?"

"I'll be carefree, sit under a tree, relax, sing songs, and bask in the sunshine."

The seated man smiled. "That's exactly what I'm doing right now!"

I understand that there is no such thing as a life without sacrifice and enjoyment follows hard work.

But are we truly looking for a soft life?

It's not that we don't want a challenge in life, it's the challenge itself that we want to change. For all our lives, the challenge meant finding our place in the system, blending in with everyone, joining the pack so our survival was ensured. It meant that we had to absorb life's predetermined protocol of how our time on Earth would play out, and we had to serve as shills to this protocol. A soft life is exactly what we want to achieve after retirement. Why not choose to prioritize community, connections, relationships, mental health, overall health *before* we retire?

Perhaps this perceived anti-ambition is the cusp of what ambition in life should mean.

Can't we reverse-engineer our lives so our foundation is stronger and our careers serve as a positive externality of that rock-solid grounding? Can't we choose mindfully to live a life that puts our well-being first and the rest second?

What would the world look like if our work were a result of how we feel about life, rather than how we feel as a result of our work?

I believe our ambitions would improve tenfold. When we no longer rely on our weekends to catch up with our favorite activities, meeting new people, building relationships, engaging in our craft, enjoying the sunshine, and pursuing our creative passions— the aftermath that emerges from that engagement will build a better world for all of us.

This would be a drastic shock to our system, of course. We would be building a society based on sincere, creative pursuits rather than transactional, mechanical routines. We would strip away all the deception from the system and build an entirely new one based on what we love. Plus, when we awaken to the realization that career does not equal life, we put into practice some of our deepest traits as a collective species that have evolved for millions of years. We can and want to take care of each other.

When we work at jobs that drain our energy, we inevitably become an atomized society based on animosity and skepticism. No one has the energy to collaborate, communicate or cooperate with one another. We would rather rest and charge up like machines waiting for our next shift.

And when we treat our career as a function of our life and how we honor our time on Earth, we also awaken to a deeper realization: we are nothing without others.

In one email to himself, Steve Jobs described how he would be nothing without his tribe:

"I did not breed or perfect the seeds. I do not make any of my own clothing. I speak a language I did not invent or refine. I did not discover the mathematics I use. I am protected by freedoms and laws I did not conceive of or legislate and do not enforce or adjudicate. I am moved by music I did not create myself. When I needed medical attention, I was helpless to help myself survive. I did not invent the transistor, the microprocessor, object-oriented programming, or most of the technology I work with. I love and admire my species, living and dead, and am totally dependent on them for my life and well-being.

Sent from my iPad."[4]

When we are inside the hamster wheel, we constantly forget how amazing and awe-fueling our species is, and how much we need and rely on one another. I wrote these words on a computer I didn't make, on a software program I didn't create sitting in a building I didn't build, drinking a coffee I didn't make, speaking and expressing thoughts with words I didn't create.

Our greatness is only a function of our collective greatness. We stand on the shoulders of giants! We depend on each other more than we think. That realization becomes crystal clear when we have time to expand the size and scope of our time on Earth, and can reflect on the things that truly matter, such as giving back to our community.

Repairing the World

Tikun Olam is an ancient Jewish concept that translates into "Repairing the World." It states that all of us have a responsibility to repair and improve the world, which is deeply entrenched in our nature as a species. Given that we are the leaders of nature, we have a sense of agency in life, and these actions lead us to finding long-lasting fulfillment.

Nicholas Christakis, a brilliant sociologist and professor of Social and Natural Science at Yale University and previous guest on my podcast[5], studies how our species is wired for goodness. Professor Christakis is the author of several books, including one of my favorites of all time, *Blueprint: The Evolutionary Origins of a Good Society.*[6] Christakis argues that our social nature, which includes our capacity for empathy and cooperation, is encoded in our evolutionary history. He argues that, without our capacity for cooperation, we would not have been able to thrive as a species.[7]

In his book, he points to evidence that suggests when cultures are built upon the values of working together to accomplish complex tasks, sharing resources with one another, and taking responsibility for the young and elderly, they tend to thrive more than cultures based on violence, animosity, and aggression. Of course, Christakis acknowledges that we are also capable of violence, but everything points to the fact that our nature is one of cooperation and kindness.[8]

There are several moral values that most societies share between them, and this universality is further evidence of a shared human nature that values cooperation, fairness, and empathy. One example is the "golden rule" which states that we should treat others as we would like to be treated, a value that Confucianism coins as *ren* which derives from Confucius' statement, "What you don't want done to yourself, do not do to others." In Hinduism, the concept of *ahimsa* or non-violence is a core principle: treat others with compassion and never engage in violent actions. In Judaism, the Hebrew Bible contains a verse that says, "Love your neighbor as yourself" and in Islam, the prophet Muhammad is reported to have said, "None of you believes until he lives for his brother what he loves for himself." For Christakis, this universality proves that our nature is embedded with love and cooperation.

In the field of neuroscience, strong evidence exists that our brain is designed to incentivize cooperation with each other: When we help others, our brains release certain chemicals such as Dopamine and Oxytocin, which are linked with prosocial behaviors and positive emotions.[9]

Known as the "helper's high," many people commit their lives to altruism due to the positive feelings they receive from acts of kindness.[10] Further, Christakis argues that this positive response happens when we help others beyond our own social group. Studies have shown that people feel pleasure when they see strangers helping strangers, further strengthening his argument that our capacity for empathy and altruism is not limited to our tribe, but to all members of our species.[11]

There's a reason why acts of kindness go viral in social media—as a species, we love to see good things happen to our fellow humans. However, when we are caught up in an empty chase, we don't have the luxury to reflect on how we can be a force for good and the responsibility we have to heal the world.

So, when people start living an "anti-ambitious" life that prioritizes their well-being and values their life over their careers, the individualistic chase for greatness ceases to exist, and the void becomes filled with a deeper sense of community.

Dar LaBeach, a once-successful marketing professional who made up to $150,000 a year, decided to make a drastic change in his life when he was laid off during the pandemic.[12]

While working, he reported feeling stressed, anxious, disenchanted, and 'tired of living for others' rather than himself. He suddenly realized that life could be more than feeling drained as a result of his job, regardless of the money left over on the table. His decision allowed him to travel more and have a career simultaneously without allowing his career to dominate his life. [13]

LaBeach traveled to Mexico, and slowly began to realize that he had a keen sense of community and helping others. He began to become involved in social activism, helping to raise awareness of women's rights, and regardless of how small the community was, he wanted to be actively involved. [14]

When we start taking care of ourselves by listening to what we truly need, goodness kicks in, even if our actions initially seem self-centered. When we allow space between us and our preconceived notions of what life should look like, we allow our truest feelings and intuitions to emerge. When we act in such "a selfish manner," we are paradoxically acting in the most selfless way we can. Sometimes, when we allow time to reveal the answers to us and give ourselves enough cushion to find what moves us, we can then move forward and start healing the world because our gas tank is filled with positivity.

Sometimes, all we really need to heal is space to prioritize our well-being—and remember that by "well-being" I mean deciding to live an authentic life. The mindful quest enables us to discover the door to which *we* are the key.

No, I don't believe I am arguing in favor of living a life without unpleasant situations and challenges. On the contrary, I believe that hard work pays off and that good fortune comes to those willing to sacrifice. I'm advocating for authenticity. Choosing what *we* want to sacrifice, on our terms. I am offering a new set of tools to evaluate the hidden costs of our choices to give us a much-needed perspective on our decisions and their consequences.

Remember: society sells the benefit but fails to disclose the cost. We are slowly waking up to the idea that it is not worth the costs of living an inauthentic life for the sake of a paycheck, praise, or a promotion. We are unwilling to sacrifice our youth just to keep an economic machine going. This trade is more than unfair—it is a crime against our time on Earth.

We are waking up, but we still need an extra push. We still live on autopilot, cruising through two-thirds of our lives just because we were sold the stability card. For creators, that formula will never fulfill us.

Older generations had it drilled into them that part of living a rewarding life means to sacrifice, often including their own thoughts and emotions. Some are even willing to sacrifice their own sense of self. I believe that we can change the course. There is no sense in buying the goods without asking for the costs, and I am not referring to financial costs. Being wealthy is very costly, being conventionally successful—against your true self—is very costly.

Prioritizing your own genuine ambitions, rather than society's, is perhaps the most ambitious and fulfilling goal we can aim for.

A Cosmic Meditation on Life and Work

If the path before you is clear, you're probably on someone else's.

When the astrophysicist Neil deGrasse Tyson was in college, he was part of the wrestling team. His closest teammate was two years older than him. One day, the two were walking out of practice, and his friend asked him, "What are you majoring in again?"

Neil answered, "Astrophysics."

His friend, surprised with Neil's answer said, "The black community cannot afford the luxury of someone with your intellect becoming an astrophysicist."

His friend was majoring in economics and went on to become a Rhodes scholar.

In Neil's words:

> "...that was a very heavy emotional burden he put on me, that one sentence, because I knew, intellectually, he was correct, but emotionally it's not what I felt. Emotionally, I loved the universe. I wanted to study the universe."[15]

Adding to his emotional burden, his father, Cyril deGrasse Tyson, was a social activist who led anti-poverty programs in New York City and worked to improve the city's education system. He had built a career in social urban policy with the goal of empowering disadvantaged communities. Tyson's father was an ardent proponent of promoting social equity and held a firm conviction that education played a crucial role in disrupting the cycle of poverty. He dedicated himself relentlessly to enhancing the educational standards in New York City, actively championing initiatives aimed at offering job training and other prospects to individuals from marginalized backgrounds.

Being raised by such an exemplary individual in the social rights movement, Neil also felt pressured to find a way of bringing justice to the world. Neil describes feeling the emotional burden of whether to follow his heart up until graduate school.[16]

But a serendipitous break for his interest in the cosmos came for Neil. In 1989, he was invited for an interview on a local New York TV station to discuss a plasma burst, and after he finished the pre-recorded interview, he went home, re-watched the tape, and came to an eye-opening realization:

> "I'd never before in my life seen an interview with a black person on television solely for their expertise unrelated to their racial background."[17]

Imagine! That was the first time Neil had ever seen a black person answering questions about his expertise and not about his race.

At that moment, Neil deGrasse Tyson became a trailblazer for the black community. He opened the door for them to envision themselves as experts, leading voices in their field of choice—not pigeonholed by their racial background.

When Neil followed his heart, he created social justice in an unintended way. Just for a second, imagine that Neil would have chosen to become an economist or an acceptable path by his friend. Sure, someone as smart as he would have made inroads in any other field, but his genuine impact came from following his heart rather than his mind—putting his intellect to work to manifest his heart's desire which was to explore the universe and share his insights with all of us, sparking awe for our cosmos. By following his true calling, he channeled his father's push for social justice in ways that nobody expected.

In his book, *Starry Messenger: Cosmic Perspectives on Civilization*, Neil begins with the following quote by Edgar D. Mitchell, Apollo 14 Astronaut:

> "You develop an instant global consciousness, a people orientation, an intense dissatisfaction with the state of the world, and a compulsion to do something about it. From out there on the Moon, international politics look so petty. You want to grab a politician by the scruff of the neck and drag him a quarter of a million miles out and say, 'Look at that, you son of a bitch.'"[18]

When astronauts fly to space, they experience a drastic shift in their consciousness. This phenomenon is called the "Overview Effect," a cognitive shift that strikes them with overwhelming emotions of connectedness to all life on Earth when they see our blue home from space.[19] Researcher's describe it as "a state of awe with self-transcendent qualities, precipitated by a particularly striking visual stimulus."[20]

They are not only overwhelmed by this newfound *connectedness* to our home, but to other people as well.

Why is it that we desire to explore space and push the boundaries of what is possible, both in terms of technological innovation and our potential to become an interplanetary species? Why are we so eager to go to space, explore new planets—and perhaps colonize Mars—when here on Earth, we face numerous challenges?

These questions made me think about what Neil said about space exploration, which is counterintuitive to what I ever thought would happen once we fly outside our planet.

> "...the first Earth Day was created in 1970, while we were going to the Moon. And when we arrived, we looked back over our shoulders and discovered Earth for the first time."[21]

In other words, we landed on the Moon only to discover Earth for the first time. What a profound insight.

In his book, Neil describes how the 1969 Apollo 11 missions changed our perspective on Earth and, in turn, our treatment of it:[22]

• Apollo 11 (First to walk on the Moon) was in 1969

• The National Oceanic and Atmospheric Administration (NOAA) was formed in 1970

• The First National Earth Day was established in 1970

• The Environmental Protection Agency (EPA) was formed in 1970

• The Clean Water Act was passed in 1972

Going to space allowed us to see the treasure we already hold here on Earth, and led us to create policies to preserve it. So, while the immediate conclusion about going to space might be that it will make us fall in love with our universe, the truth is that it opens our eyes to how astonishing and unique the tiny blue marble we call our home is.

How could the Overview Effect affect our perspective of our time on Earth?

Although I have not experienced it firsthand, reading Dr. Tyson's *Starry Messenger* enabled me to imagine myself in outer space, having some sort of an out-of-body meditative experience in which I could see the Earth from far beyond the cosmos.

In this "cosmic meditation," I focused my attention on what my conventional life looked like from outer space: a daily, almost robotic routine, with a touch of desire to impress others through my titles and career achievements, my need for approval, which at times came at the expense of my own approval.

By pushing our imagination to envision ourselves from outer space, we can put a lot of the things that matter in life in perspective. It helps us remove the notion that the prime reason for why we are alive is to achieve something.

What is real when we look back on Planet Earth from outer space, is how almost all of these imagined systems, including our existing political, economic, and social systems, have had a tangible impact on our world: We have drawn imaginary border lines that divide two "different" types of people, often resulting in a deadly tug of war for resources. We have extracted some of the rarest resources from nature to fulfill a quota on a company's balance sheet so those who own shares of said company make profits, leaving a trail of lifeless destruction within our forests, our mountains, and our oceans.

What struck me most profoundly when I envisioned myself floating in outer space (if you were wondering, no, I was not on a mushroom trip) is that, while all the imaginary systems are just that—*imaginary*—we hold a godlike power to make them real. We are capable of building empires based on an ideology, and we have just as much power to destroy them. We are capable of embracing an imaginary idea, such as a nation, that can unite an entire group of people, and we are just as capable of using this same idea to divide, resent, and even hate each other.

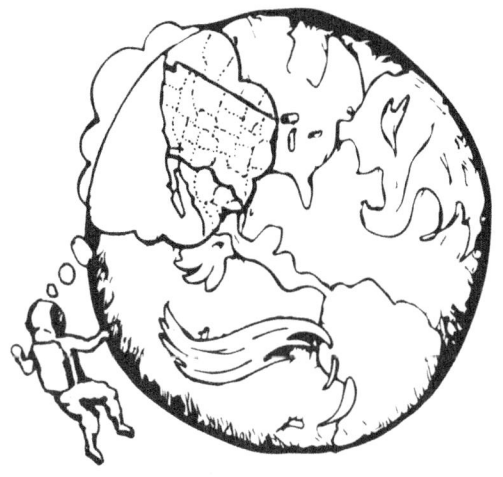

We are capable of adopting a concept, such as the industrial-style design of work, to shape our entire existence on our planet as if it were a natural law, like gravity, and we create entire lives based on it.

But we too have the powerful capacity to realize how these concepts are just that—*concepts*.

We can realize that, while these imaginary systems have yielded results in the past, they are not immovable forces of our reality, and we can adapt them to serve us rather than rob us of our humanity, our creativity, and our connection to our planet and to our people.

We have just as much power to self-correct, change course, build new concepts, and ask new questions about what work really means, such as the following:

• In our new era, one heavily driven by technology, how can we envision work that relies more on our creativity than on grunt activity?

• How can we build a life in synchronicity with nature's rhythms rather than setting ourselves at odds with them?

• What if, instead of neglecting our creative nature, we embrace it?

Perhaps Neil didn't write his book on cosmic perspectives thinking it would induce an out of body experience within his readers, but I'm thankful I had that experience. It got me thinking about my hubris and self-aggrandizing perspective that I was the most important piece of the solar system, and how leading a life with this idea was robbing me of discovering aspects of my elevated humanity. I realized I have been committing a crime against my own humanity by living a life on autopilot, trying to chase senseless awards, titles, or prestige, and running the risk of spending my entire adult life trying to prove how worthy I am in the eyes of others.

It is almost impossible not to empathize with our fellow astronauts and not be washed over by overwhelming emotions of compassion toward others, coupled with a deepened love for our home.

Envisioning ourselves floating in space while staring back at our tiny little blue marble, buoyant in a vast, infinite dark ocean that is the universe, can be a jarring experience. What's striking about this is that the tiny blue marble stares back at us with all its might, its vibrant blue and green contrasting colors providing us with a glimpse of what we never thought we would witness: perfection.

When I try to absorb the words of the brilliant astrophysicist and the late astronaut Edgar Mitchell, I cannot help but feel some sense of guilt and absurdity when I think about the games I played up until I decided to write this book. While trying to chase senseless objectives tied up with a conventional definition of success, I found myself isolated from my family and friends and deeply disconnected from my planet and my people. Moreover, I realized that chasing grandiosity just for the sake of grandiosity in any field, any career, was pointless to the point where it does a disservice to how unique our planet is.

When we realize that we are living inside the only proven authentic, perfect thing in the universe, it is unfathomable to accept the feelings of disconnectedness, loneliness, and greed as the natural paths we should embrace. It just makes no sense.

What does make sense, however, is honoring our time on Earth by exploring and embracing our creative nature. The only positive sum game we can play is the creative one, which aligns with the overwhelming, optimistic feelings that run through the astronauts' veins when they see the Earth from above. When we explore our creative nature—and act upon it—I believe we tap into the Overview Effect.

When I write these words, which are an expression of my creativity, I feel a deep, humbled connection to my planet. I think about you, my reader, and become washed over with feelings of empathy, appreciation, and compassion toward you because you, too, are a creative astronaut who just so happens to be on board the spaceship we call Earth with a spacesuit we call the human body.

It just so happens that you, like me, were born into this world without a guide or a recipe for living. You, like me, are trying to connect with your creative potential and tap into your innermost sanctum that you feel will contribute to the canvas of our spaceship. You, like me, are reading these words and experiencing perhaps inspiration, exhilaration, and a refined sense of how you see your time cruising aboard this tiny, yet massive, little blue marble.

When we tap into our creative nature, we invigorate the world and provide it with new life. While it is true that we are alive for a very short time compared to cosmic time—a good one hundred years (knock on wood)—these years can be packed with joy, optimism, kindness, and love toward ourselves and others.

Yes, I hear you saying that this chapter is the most "kumbaya" thus far, but I believe that we need to act more from this side of the equation and start to rid ourselves of the perspective that our time on Earth is only for paying bills and waiting to live and enjoy the sunshine until retirement (which implies that being alive does not matter).

As a species, we face several collective challenges, including climate change, political division, and rising inequality. Even though I wish I had a magic wand to solve all these issues once and for all, I don't. But having a cosmic perspective of our time on Earth is the closest we have to a magic wand, as it adds a sense of urgency to sort out our problems and differences—and connects us to one another in ways we have never experienced before.

Cosmic Meditation

As we are arriving at the last parts of this chapter, I invite you to try out this exercise of the "cosmic meditation." Make sure you are in a place where you can relax, take a couple of deep breaths, close your eyes, and envision yourself floating in outer space while looking back on your home, Planet Earth, and feel as if you just discovered it for the first time. Imagine yourself floating like a feather, light as air, while Earth looks back at you.

Think about how you feel as her undeniable beauty strikes your eyes, and submerge deep within yourself and reflect.

What does it spark within you? What emotions do you feel emerge within you?

What thoughts does seeing your home for the first time evoke within you?

Do you feel awestruck, overwhelmed, inspired? Try to settle into these emotions and let yourself relax naturally.

Consider bringing your attention to your own experience being alive, at least for a brief moment.

What does your relationship between your home and yourself look like?

Do you feel connected to it?

Do you feel connected to your neighbors?

How do you feel about your relationship with work and your career?

How do you feel about how you're honoring your time on Earth?

Are you painting our blue and green home's canvas with your true colors and creative nature?

Now that you have reflected on these deep and intimate questions, perhaps you want to write them down, along with your thoughts. Also, consider the idea that these feelings *are* the answers themselves. Sometimes, there is no need to put into words or rationalize what happened within you—at least for now. Sometimes, our emotions are the answer we are looking for.

As time passes by, try to envision a life built around the reflections you had while floating in outer space. See what your life would look like. See what your relationship with work could look like. But, perhaps most importantly, see what your Time on Earth could look like.

It is estimated that by 2025, we will be able to land on the Moon again.[23] And several companies are already offering pre-sale tickets to fly to space—though they remain costlier than the word costly.[24]

Nonetheless, while we can't yet experience the Overview Effect on a collective scale, we can envision ourselves in space, reflecting on how much justice we are doing to our time on Earth and how much we have truly painted on its canvas.

I invite you to stay curious and creative—and keep looking up.

Pause and Ponder: Chapter Eight

• How can I incorporate aspects of a "soft life" into my current routine, even in small ways?

• Try the "cosmic meditation," then sit with your thoughts and feelings. Write down the first thing that comes to mind—no filter.

• In our tech-driven era, how can I envision work that leverages my creativity rather than monotonous, repetitive tasks?

• How can I align my life with nature's rhythms instead of working against them?

• What would it look like if I embraced my creative nature instead of neglecting it?

PART III

ACTION

'In 1912 Jung published a book in which he said in strong language,

"The spirit of evil is the negation of the life force by fear. Only boldness can deliver us from fear. If the risk is not taken, the meaning of life is violated."

I've said to people, if you type that up and put it on your bathroom mirror and you look at it every day, you're going to become a little more mindful of the role that fear, typically through avoidance, is running your life.

Don't judge the fear. Recognize that you also, as a conscious being, have an agenda to expand your life in the face of that fear.'

— JAMES HOLLIS

9

THE ART OF CATCHING SERENDIPITY

If you do not trust life to unfold, the mind takes over and it becomes a game of strategy, motivated by anxiety. This mistrust is unfair. Life has given us so much, and yet we do not trust it.

— *MOOJI*

To truly excel as individuals, we often mistakenly believe that we must relentlessly chase after goals with all our energy. In reality, this single-minded pursuit can lead us astray from genuine fulfillment. It is true that when we set our sights on a fixed objective and navigate our lives through hard work, we might feel satisfaction and fulfillment. But this feeling only lasts *less than* half a breath, which explains why so many people are quite *literally addicted* to always chasing the next "big thing" in their lives.

When we obsess over reaching any given milestone—graduating, getting promoted, receiving an award—we also falsely think that we must mute everything along the road between us and that destination. We tend to think of those things, such as our inner hearts whispers as distractions and possible detours from reaching our initial goal.

I know many of you reading these words might have a difficult time reconciling the idea of setting an objective and being sufficiently open-minded, almost being willing to be "distracted" on the road to achieving your goal. Believe me, it took me a long time to digest this idea, and during my time working at my "dream job," I forfeited opportunities of building new relationships, getting into deep conversations, attending social events, and participating in community-building. I stubbornly thought that any kind of interaction indirectly related to my job would, potentially, derail and steer me in the wrong direction.

However, I now see things in a completely different light. Those opportunities were the direct result of my deliberate intention to set a goal for myself, and those opportunities were the gems along the road.

Let me illustrate this idea in the following way:

Let's say you go fishing; you have your fishing line, hook, and bait. The goal is to catch a fish, any fish. Knowing exactly what you'll catch can diminish the excitement—part of the thrill lies in the unpredictability of the outcome.

Let's think of the fishing line as the representation of the path between you and your goal. Sometimes you throw the line very far, sometimes very close depending on the range of your fishing line—it could be short, medium, or long-term *ended*. The hook with the bait serves as the *attractor* between you and your goal, the ocean represents the vast space of opportunity that you can achieve as you chase your objective, and the fish is the surprising reward after your journey.

Fishing is quite literally the physical representation of jumping into the endless, magical universe of serendipity.

Any goal in our lives has symbolically the same meaning: The goal is a path that gives us a clear purpose and vision, it allows us to aim toward something. We realistically orient ourselves to begin walking in the direction of our destination, and we therefore have enough certainty to take the first step forward. The catch here, which is where we find the biggest rewards in life, is to exercise our muscle of flexibility and open-mindedness about surprising detours along our road while making sure these golden nuggets across our path are detected by our intuition, and leveraging our internal compass to tell us what "detours" feel right for us.

In short, our goals provide a starting point, but they shouldn't be considered the endgame.

Focusing solely on achieving goals can lead to a sense of emptiness once they are reached. Separation between the feeling and reality kicks in: "[sigh] I achieved everything I ever wanted. Then why do I feel this way? [followed by an even longer, more disheartened sigh]." We're not built to become so fixated on one thing so much that we discard serendipity as the ultimate reward along the journey.

We don't allow the fish to catch our bait. Rather, our bait catches the fish because we have been told to "fix" the plot twists in our lives, to force things, rather than to embrace the twists and turns in our path. We've mechanized our lives in such a way that we have conditioned ourselves to believe that life is best lived through formulas and recipes that emerge from the rational mind. We are told from a very young age to start thinking about what we want to do when we grow up, and as we begin to grow older and our peers begin asking, "What is your plan?" We are forced to answer rationally with a detailed goal so as to prevent social embarrassment and the typical answer, "You can't live on that, that career does not pay money," or "that's not a legitimate goal—think again."

A great example of setting a goal and letting our intuition carve the path is Elvis Presley. Elvis' journey to fame began with a simple intention to record songs as a gift for his mother, not to achieve overnight success.[1]

When he was eighteen years old, he went to the offices of Sun Records in Memphis, Tennessee, hoping to record a couple of songs for his mother as a gift. As Elvis began singing, Sam Phillips, the owner of Sun Records, was taken back by his voice and asked him to come back more often and record songs for him. His first single, "That's All Right," became an instant local hit.

This serendipitous moment, rather than a fabricated one, propelled his career forward.

Even though Elvis set his sights on becoming a singer, he did not follow a prescribed path to do so. He just followed the leads his path offered and what his intuition caught along the road, allowing serendipity to guide his journey. If he would have chosen to follow a rational recipe to achieve his goals, he would have never dared to walk into Sun Records solely intending to record some songs for her mother. Instead, he would have gone into Sam's offices, quite nervously given that he would presumably be focused on achieving his objective (making him susceptible to playing to not lose rather than playing to win), and asked to be trained as a singer or even request an internship.

Initially, his intention was not to become an overnight success. He just wanted to give his mother a gift. But serendipity entered the room, and Sam offered him an opportunity to explore his talent.

For Elvis, the fish caught the bait. You must allow this to happen.

You must allow the fish to catch your bait.

When we follow our passions for the sake of following them, serendipity takes charge, and we send a signal to the universe that brings us closer to discovering our true potential. The less we focus our sights on achieving one goal, one grand vision, the closer we are to achieving it.

The more we focus on trying to reach our goals, the more they elude us.

What Artificial Intelligence Teaches Us About Life and Greatness

> Greatness can only be achieved if you stop demanding what that greatness should be.
>
> — *KENNETH STANLEY*

In their provocative book, *Greatness Cannot Be Planned: The Myth of the Objective*, Joel Lehman and Kenneth O. Stanley turned the world of the conventional hustle-mindset upside down, arguing that objective-based living is by far the worst strategy we can choose if we have set our sights to achieving greatness.[2]

For me, the book was an eye-opener, articulating what I've felt for a long time now and have written throughout these pages: We are not built to live a scripted, goal-oriented life. We are not built to reach greatness by following a linear path towards our "dreams."

In reality, these grandiose dreams bring us further and further from our visions and ultimately, distance us from long-lasting fulfillment in our lives. How can such a thing happen? How is it the case that the more we focus on achieving any goal, the less likely it is we actually achieve it?

Even more intriguing, why is it that when someone *does reach their goal, does achieve greatness,* does get to the finish line, they feel rather depleted of energy and disappointed, often articulating words when arriving such as "is this really it"?

This happens because we are built for maximum serendipity, not for maximum optimization.

In a deeply intriguing experiment, Kenneth and Joel show how an AI robot, programmed to find novelty rather than just arrive at its destiny in the most efficient way, actually reached its objectives more rapidly.

The robot was placed inside a maze, and the purpose of the experiment was to see how quickly the robot would exit the maze, depending on its algorithm.[3]

In a series of trials, every single time the robot that was programmed to just look for novelty, without explicitly stating that the novelty was exiting the maze, it found the exit much faster than the robot specifically programmed to find the exit.[4] Mind boggling, right? Being led only by an awe-infusing program, the AI robot reached its goals faster.

This is a profound lesson for all of us: the more we try to reach our goals in a direct, literal and efficient manner, the longer it may take us to reach them—and even potentially never realizing them.

Some of the greatest athletes of all time are clear examples that mindset and goal setting are the keys to success (e.g., LeBron James and Kobe Bryant). To a certain extent, I agree. Without their mindset, they would have never achieved their goals and greatness. On the other hand, LeBron expressed a deep love for the game of basketball that goes back to when he played the sport at five years old 'on a crate,' and Bryant expressed multiple times that he was 'deeply obsessed' with basketball.[5]

These out-of-this-world athletes show how pursuing what we deeply love to do for the sake of just doing it because it feels right within ourselves actually boosts our potential to achieve greatness. Did LeBron ever say when he began shooting hoops at five years old, "I want to do this because it will bring me greatness?" Of course not, and neither did Kobe wake up one day as a child and decide how he would reach top one-percent status by becoming one of the greatest athletes of all-time.

There are far more lucrative, less demanding endeavors these men could have chosen to achieve their goals, but they achieved them by simply pursuing what they deeply loved. In other words, when pouring our hearts into a craft we are intrinsically connected to, greatness will take care of itself, regardless of its shape or form.

Perhaps you won't become the greatest point guard of all-time or the highest-grossing actor who ever lived. But if you calibrate your radar only with goal-oriented coordinates, not only will you instantly distance yourself from achieving that which you want to achieve the most, but you will completely shut the door down between yourself and the serendipitous nature of the journey—all in a fraction of milliseconds. You won't even notice, won't even know—perhaps for an entire lifetime—how magical your journey could have been.

Paradoxically, the less you focus on achieving your goals, the closer you are to achieving them. The less objective-driven your life becomes, the more your odds of success. The less mechanized a life you build, the more opportunities you will have to become inspired.

The less you chase your dream, the more likely it is that you will realize it.

The less scripted your life is, the more awe-inspiring it becomes.

No doubt, these concepts are difficult to digest, as our entire modern existence is based on goal-setting, optimizing, and careful calibration. Indeed, that is practically the modus operandi of every single human living in the modern world.

Understanding the challenge of embracing a non-goal-oriented lifestyle isn't easy for me either. Based on a personality test, I learned that I'm highly industrious and extremely conscientious —I thrive on efficiency and clear goals. So, it's quite a shift to consider that success can come more naturally to me when I stop trying so hard to achieve it. Just know that if it's tough for you to see life this way, I'm right there with you struggling with the same realization.

As Joel and Kenneth write in *Greatness Cannot Be Planned*, we have been conditioned from an early age to think of our lives as a function of who we need to become when we grow up. If you notice, most games we used to play when we were young (such as role-playing games based on who we wanted to be in the future) set us on a path to associating fulfillment, sense of purpose, and social recognition by what we can accomplish, instead of who we already are, and who can we become.[6]

Goal setting is not a natural law that should drive our lives. Artificial Intelligence has revealed that serendipity and novelty seeking play a much larger role in all the successes and paradigm-shifting discoveries than we previously thought, and provide a much better framework for living a fulfilling, creatively driven life for all of us.[7]

When we follow our interests without a hidden agenda, this is the best way of reaching greatness, and when we don't define what greatness should be, we might find it in its purest, most unconstrained, most natural form.[8]

Kenneth and Joel expand upon this idea by discussing several discoveries that have been made throughout humankind's existence, like the computer and rock and roll. The first computer, in fact, was built using vacuum tubes—devices used to 'channel electric current through a vacuum.'[9]

The strange part here, Kenneth and Joel argue, is that the creation of vacuum tubes has nothing to do with computers. Those who were working on vacuum tubes were focused on electricity, not computers. The pursuit of their interests opened the door to the advancement of computer technology.[10]

Another example is born out of a combination between jazz, gospel, blues, and country music, Kenneth and Joel write. The eureka moment here is that neither jazz, gospel, nor blues singers had the intention of creating rock and roll. The pure reality is that these artists were just being themselves, and their passion ultimately became a 'stepping stone' for rock and roll to be discovered. What's startling about these findings is that if, in the above examples, the innovators had set out to create a computer or rock and roll, they may never have achieved their goals, or they would have delayed the process, riddled with challenges for a long time.[11]

Goal setting can actually *constrain* our ability to achieve greatness. When we put on our horse blinders in the spirit of focusing on what we should achieve, we foreclose the potential stepping stones that could bring us closer to the peak of our creative potential.

In other words, when we write our recipe for success, build a checklist of steps to take along the way, and proceed to execute them, we become blind to potentially better ventures that are within our reach.

Even more surprising is that when we set goals for ourselves, we potentially send ourselves toward dead ends. Although all metrics might indicate that we are getting closer to our goals, the numbers and methodologies deceive us, and we find ourselves the furthest we've ever been from achieving them.

Imagine you're in a maze and have been programmed to reach a treasure. To evaluate your progress on whether you are getting closer to the desired destination, you use a progress bar that increases in percentage value when you approach the goal and decreases when you are farther away. You begin your quest by trying to raise the value of the progress bar, and voila, the further north you go, the closer you get to it. In fact, you reach the 99.99th percentile of closeness to your destination if you just head north. However, when you get that close to your destination, you encounter a wall between you and the treasure that you cannot traverse.[12]

That is, you are literally a step away from your treasure, but you cannot reach it—not ever.

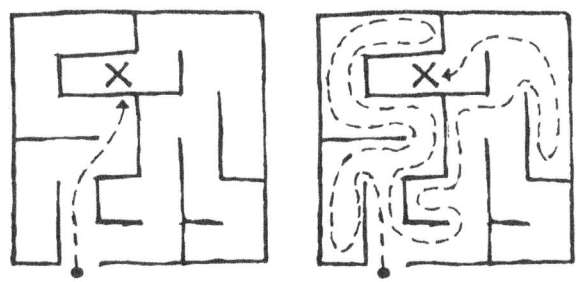

You see, the risk of goal setting is that it is extremely harmful and deceptive. Based on all the metrics, you took the best possible route and you are *literally* the closest you can be of your desired destination. Yet, you feel exhausted and frustrated because all you see is a wall, never having access to the treasure on the other side.

Now, let's say that you are programmed to search for novelty. So, the goal here is to be amazed by the maze rather than trying to solve it and get to the treasure. Let's say you take the northern route again, and you get to the same wall as before. You see this wall as a novel experience, you record it, and move on. Then, you take the eastern route, and you go through the same process. You are amazed by it and move on. Ultimately, you go through this same process for all the routes until you get to the coveted treasure!

While you were not programmed to search for the treasure, this strategy proved more useful for two reasons:

(1) you enjoyed the path for the sake of exploring the path; and

(2) you were ultimately rewarded with a treasure, thus you killed two birds with one stone.

This strategy also yields better results because pursuing novelty means we don't see obstacles as obstacles but rather as novel encounters throughout our journey.

In other words, you can—you are more likely to—achieve greatness without ever setting your sights on greatness.

Reaching greatness by defining what greatness should be is seriously constraining and harmful. If having a career packed with achievement and recognition would cut it for everyone who achieved "greatness," then all of us would attain long-lasting satisfaction by following this path, but we don't. In fact, job dissatisfaction is at an all-time high.[13]

If that were the actual definition of the term, we would not be as depressed, isolated, and stressed as we are.

If becoming a Hollywood star or a famous singer would offer a stairway to success, all actors and singers would live high quality lives, but they don't. There are countless examples of people experiencing severe depression, substance abuse, and committing suicide as they followed these coveted paths (e.g., Kurt Cobain, Anthony Bourdain, and Robin Williams). Even my favorite comedian, Jim Carrey, has dealt with depression.

Jim Carrey once gave a commencement speech for the 2014 class of the Maharishi International University of Management.[14]

In his speech, Jim took the crowd on a journey of laughter, insights, and direct truths. He essentially put this chapter's theme into one sentence:

> "I've often said that I wish people could realize all their dreams and wealth and fame so that they could see that it's not where you're going to find your sense of completion."[15]

In other words, do not allow yourself to be bound to golden cuffs that promise greatness, which, in reality, only tie you to a dead end. A true sense of completion will never manifest itself within you if you realize the mechanized dreams you design often based on wealth and success, but rather, from pursuing what emanates from inside you.

Jim goes on to describe a vital lesson his father taught him:

> "My father could have been a great comedian, but he didn't believe that that was possible for him. And so, he made a conservative choice. Instead, he got a safe job as an

accountant. And when I was twelve years old, he was let go from that safe job and our family had to do whatever we could to survive. I learned many great lessons from my father, not the least of which was that you can fail at what you don't want so you might as well take a chance on doing what you love."[16]

Our mind is an expert in deception. As discussed previously, its intention is not to con us out of our dreams and passions, but to protect us. Taking a leap of faith is the least rational choice anyone can make, especially in modernity, when the path of security has never been as attainable and as "guaranteed" as society professes.

As Jim tells us in the story of his father, we can absolutely fail at what we hate doing, so we might as well try and fail at doing what we love. On the flip side, we can succeed at doing something we hate, so why not try to succeed at something we love? It's so much more fulfilling and sustaining, after all.

It's difficult to quit something that has yielded 'great' results. In other words, we're good at playing games we don't like. We receive the promotions, the big bucks, the stability, the comfort, and the applause.

These perks are very hard to give up on, but that is precisely why they exist in the first place—to make us play broken games; to keep us hooked. That's what the money's for; that's what the comfort of the biweekly paycheck is for; that's what the applause is for.

Most of the time, we go through the motions of our work and career half-heartedly and still achieve amazing results. Now, imagine what we could accomplish if we would give all our hearts to pursuing our passions without guardrails and without feeling the dread and drudgery of our jobs!

It is worth repeating that safety, paradoxically, can be the most dangerous decision we may ever make. So, is our chase for defined greatness just a cop out for us to avoid sincerely asking ourselves what 'greatness' means to us, and starting our journey in that direction?

Are you choosing to follow a linear, mechanized path that sells you prestige, comfort, reputation, and wealth based on a place of fear or based on love?

While it's simpler to follow a pre-established path, both practically and imaginatively, the real challenge isn't just walking this path. Instead, the true test involves breaking free from predefined notions of what 'greatness' should look like, challenging the constraints and definitions that confine us.

Jim can help us close this crazy journey packed with fish, AI, and comedy:

> "When I was about twenty-eight, after a decade as a professional comedian, I realized one night in LA that the purpose of my life had always been to free people from concern, just like my dad. And when I realized this, I dubbed my new devotion the Church of Freedom from Concern, the Church of FFC. And I dedicated myself to that ministry. What's yours? How will you serve the world? What do they need that your talent can provide? That's all you have to figure out."[17]

Pause and Ponder: Chapter Nine

• When was the last time I felt as if serendipity was leading my life?

- How has following my intuition impacted my life in unexpected ways?

- How many choices have I made in my life based on fear?

- How about those decisions based on love?

- Which choices do I feel more comfortable with?

- What is my own Church of Freedom from Concern?

10

THE FREEDOM OF RISK

I choose me, I'm sorry.

— *KENDRICK LAMAR*

The Truth About Risk

We have a misguided view of what risk truly means in our lives. We believe that risky decisions mean quitting our jobs without a safety net, or buying a one-way trip to a new city without any plans. In modernity, we associate risk-prevention with bland life decisions. Many people (probably including you since you are reading this book up until now) have some hunch about what is involved in exploring a new opportunity—an entrepreneurial journey, starting your own blog, moving to an unknown location or perhaps quitting your day job altogether to take a leap of faith.

Most of us never take that leap of faith because we see it as unrealistic, naive, and risky.

Ask yourself: have you truly considered what risk means to you? Not to all the people around you. Not based on what others tell you but to you?

When I asked myself that question, I realized that my definition of risk wasn't really my own. It was a concept I had adopted from others, including my parents, friends, and social circle. They would define career risk as not taking the necessary steps to climb the corporate ladder. To them, risk is a tradeoff between sacrificing what they loved doing and trying to make a name for themselves.

This definition, however rational and sensible, did not resonate with me. In fact, it bothered me a lot. The concept of "eating shit" for years just to build a reputation, earn a decent salary, and have stability doing something I didn't necessarily love sounded like a complete scam and waste of my most valuable asset, my time.

So, I traveled through time to eighty-year-old me and asked that version of me myself, *what should risk mean to a twenty-something-year-old?* Should risk mean continuing to pursue a path that, while promising a respectable trajectory with financial and reputational potential, ultimately leaves me drained, tainted, and discouraged—just so I can one day *hopefully* pursue what I truly love? Or, should risk mean following my intuition, taking a leap of faith—regardless of how painful that might feel—to explore my humanity to the fullest?

Deep down, I believe you too have the answer to that question. When considering what risk means to you, reflect on how it feels to conform to traditional work roles—sitting at a lifeless desk, wearing a façade in the form of a suit and tie to please your bosses, and seeking constant promotions. Contrast this with the idea of committing wholeheartedly to your own vision, building a life you truly desire, irrespective of your current financial status, network, or the uncertainties that come with forging a new path based on intuition rather than routine.

If the answer for you is to build the conventional path by all means, go for it. It's your choice, your life. I am not demonizing any path whatsoever, as long as it comes from your core self.

But, allow me to share a cutthroat advice by Steve Jobs:

> "Don't be a career. The enemy of most dreams and intuitions, and one of the most dangerous and stifling concepts ever invented by humans, is the "Career."
>
> A career is a concept for how one is supposed to progress through stages during the training for and practicing of your working life. There are some big problems here.
>
> First and foremost is the notion that your work is different and separate from the rest of your life. If you are passionate about your life and your work, this can't be so.
>
> They will become more or less one. This is a much better way to live one's life. Make your avocation your vocation. Make what you love your work."[1]

The answer to what risk means for you will probably make you uncomfortable, it did so for me. Once I had my answer, I couldn't wait another moment. I fully understood that I would not find my true calling by procrastinating and disregarding my feelings. I would not find my true calling organizing my life through a "work-life" balance equation. The risk of waiting until "the time was right" rather than realize that "The Time Is Now" to pursue my passions was a thousand-fold more dangerous than quitting my job.

As you read this, I ask you to consider these questions based on how you think about your time on Earth:

• Have the years just "gone by" for you in a blink of an eye?

• Is time moving much more rapidly as you age?

• Do you want to pursue things for the sake of them but feel hesitant because there is no clear path toward doing so, and the financial penalty could be too high?

• Would any of this matter if you were eighty years old?

The price of regret is much higher than the cost of failure. If you, like me, have felt drained by your day job, understand that this exhaustion isn't a natural part of the human condition—it's something society has conditioned us to accept. Feeling perpetually depleted by work is not inevitable; it's a sign that something needs to change. That we need to change.

There is a clear difference between feeling exhausted from pursuing your dreams and feeling like a dried-up raisin, left without any energy to love others, the world, and yourself; there is a stark difference between feeling tethered to an imaginary responsibility and feeling liberated by your own intuition and your own definition of how you should live your life. Just because everyone feels despair does not mean it defines the human condition.

When I expressed to someone close to me that feeling drained from my job was the clearest indicator that the path I was taking was not for me, he replied, "It's not a good aspect of work for sure, but it is a natural part of it—the good ol' struggle."

We, as a society, have confused and conflicting feelings. We can feel exhausted from following our dreams but this is not the same as feeling depleted of life from our jobs. I'm not saying struggle shouldn't be a part of life. It would be stupid and reckless to think that way. I'm saying that feeling depleted of energy from working on something we don't love is not natural, and we should question that feeling. The struggle will always be a part of life and is a part of what makes it so special. However, feeling drained is a very dangerous symptom of doing something we don't love—not a necessary symptom of living.

When we follow our hearts, the failures that come from taking a real risk in life begin to be seen as lessons. They start to be perceived as a natural, fun, and dynamic part of our journey. Failures, in that sense, are detached from their negative connotation. When we follow our intuition, we actively seek to fail because it reveals the most precious gems of wisdom and provides ultimate satisfaction once overcome. We can realize life is all about failing at something we love, rather than slaving away at something we hate while time passes us by.

So, after you dialogue with your eighty-year-old self and ask the tough questions discussed in this chapter, ask yourself again: what does risk mean to you? Are you willing to pay the price of never actually *risking* anything in your life?

———

Taking That Leap of Faith

> The leap of faith is not about believing you can fly. It's about believing that something more powerful than you will catch you.
>
> —*JODI PICOULT*

When we postpone what our intuition wants us to pursue right now, we signal both to ourselves and the universe that we are not willing to put forth our most sincere, most creative work on Earth's canvas yet.

When I started writing this chapter, it was the day after my resignation from what I once thought was my dream career. The first thing that comes to mind is, "Wow, I thought there wasn't an 'after' after quitting." I genuinely believed that if I'd quit, I'd be sucked into a dark void of meaninglessness. The most significant insight I can offer you if this situation makes you afraid is this: There is no dark void, and meaning in life becomes bigger than ever. That is, of course, if you made the decision by following your heart and you allow special things to emerge.

When you take a leap of faith, life will test whether you are serious enough to finally follow your heart. Just when I was about to quit, I received a text message from my former boss praising me for the job I had done during that day. Mind you, he still did not know that I had made the decision to quit. The timing of his message felt like a cosmic test: Right then and there, I could have snapped back to my manufactured self—and I was very tempted to do it. I had reached a turning point in my career, my boss had finally texted me to congratulate me on what a great job I did— meaning a potential promotion or more responsibility could arrive. More social approval was potentially on the way. More stability...more food for my ego.

If I had not identified these situations as tests of courage from life, I would have probably returned to the office the next day and revoked my resignation letter. However, my intuition told me this was a test, and throughout that entire week, these cosmic messages kept appearing.

I am a big fan of Kendrick Lamar. "Mirror" is one song, in particular, that has been on repeat in my playlist (this was written before the Kendrick vs. Drake diss, by the way), and I've been listening to it since I began writing this book. It's the unofficial soundtrack.[2]

Kendrick sings about how he was struggling with what he was expected to do by others versus what he believed was best for him:

"I can't live in the Matrix, rather fall short of your graces."

Throughout his entire album, *Mr. Morale & Big Steppers*, he candidly admits that he cannot continue to live according to the unrealistic ideal of being a role model or a leader people have bestowed upon him—and that he has bestowed upon himself.

This Matrix in which Kendrick lives is a façade and a burden of responsibility he no longer wishes to carry and then he courageously accepts the consequences of no longer serving as the role model for his community; he no longer wishes to reinforce a mask he can't identify with anymore—and he is strong enough to maintain the separation between his mask and his true self.

Kendrick, while being one of the most influential rappers of all time, slowly adopted the role of savior. The mask was wearing him down. He admits that the end was justifying the means—selfish behavior, toxic personality, infidelity, and egoistic patterns were just a way to realize his role as savior, and as long as he was the hero, any action he made was justified. In "Mirror," he admits that therapy was a pivotal factor in his healing process and his profound realization that the savior complex was tearing him down and putting a ceiling on his actual potential (which is crazy to say when you're seen by many as one of the leading voices of a whole artistic generation).

In his song, the chorus is simple yet captures the essence of this book:

"I choose me, I'm sorry."

He says it ten times: "I choose me, I'm sorry." It is crazy—and powerful—that he felt deep within him that his own journey and self-discovery was more impactful than any expectations people may have had from him. What's crazier is that while Kendrick embarks on his own path, he continues to fulfill the role of a leader, changing lives and inspiring millions as he expresses his true colors.

The day after I finally quit my job, I was told my departure from the office was an "ongoing discussion," and they might be able to offer me a new role more tailored to my strengths. The idea appealed to my greedy ego and safe-seeking side. I could have a role in my "dream job," not disappoint my family, and continue to carve a linear path toward success. In short, I could stop myself from taking a real risk, and continue on the default path to the elusive "greatness."

I was inclined to express my interest in this new role but decided to step out of the office to clear my mind—and grab some lunch because I was starving.

I called my brother, told him about the situation, and parked for maybe ten minutes to speak with him and listen to his advice. When we finished our call, I entered the restaurant, and guess which song was playing in the background?

"Mirror" by Kendrick Lamar, with the chorus, resounding in my ears.

My heart pounded. I knew right then and there this was a cosmic message. My *Spidey* senses activated, and my spine tingled.

There was no need for confirmation—the message was right there. Had I entered the restaurant a few moments earlier, the chorus would not be playing. Had I stayed in the car a few more minutes talking with my brother, I would have missed the song. The timing was perfect.

Right then and there, I knew my path was already in motion, and the only thing missing was to say to others' expectations, to the pressure overtaking me, to the Matrix, and to my own self:

"I choose me, I'm sorry."

When to Drop the Mic

If I'm Betting on Myself I Completely Double Down

— J. COLE

If quitting is a defense mechanism to stop you from discovering your true self, then taking the leap of faith makes no sense. In other words, if quitting is based on fear and not love, not intuition, then quitting should not be considered the answer. If you believe deep within yourself that the move is aligned with your true self, and you wish to give yourself some space to allow your true colors to emerge, then believe me when I say that the universe will be your ally during this journey.

What feels so daunting about taking that leap of faith is that for the first time, you are betting solely on yourself. Whether it's leaving an unfulfilling job, starting a passion project, or pursuing a completely different path, you stop looking for permission to spread your wings and discover what kind of person you truly are.

The real reason why almost no one takes that leap of faith is because there is no script attached to it. You might have heard this cliché before: There is absolutely no one on Earth that has ever lived—or will ever live—with your identical DNA. It's true. No one in this world will ever see the world as you see it, and no one has ever been you in the most literal sense—no two people on this Earth have the same fingerprint.

The likelihood of two people sharing identical fingerprints by chance is estimated to be less than one in sixty-four billion. This means that it is more likely that a person will be struck by lightning twice than that they will have the same fingerprints as someone else. This includes identical twins![3]

The most difficult thing in life is figuring out who you are, because there is no recipe for it. Why? Because no one in the history of planet Earth has ever been you. While there are many recipes and prescriptions from gurus telling you how to find yourself, only you know—can know—who you are. Yes, you can follow specific prescriptions to guide you on an introspective journey, but your most sincere path will only arise from within you. This process is so difficult and rare that most people never dare to engage in it.

The fact that there is no script to follow makes the process uncertain, therefore perceived as risky.

But **The Time Is Now** to find out who you really are.

It's time to find out how you can make a dent in our universe. This will never happen by running through the motions like everyone else, getting a job like everyone else, or chasing the money—the applause—like everyone else. It's time for you to express yourself in this universe.

It's true, the cost of committing to this path is high. It may involve your reputation, it may involve your name, it may involve your ego.

But the cost of not doing it is higher. It will definitely involve your soul.

There has never been a better time to follow your intuition and take that leap of faith. The universe is eager to support those who follow their hearts, given the scarcity of such individuals. There's a significant disparity between the number of people who genuinely pursue their passions and the opportunities available for such pursuits. In other words, the supply of serendipity is higher than the demand. As a result, those who take that leap of faith and follow their true desires often find that the universe rapidly conspires to help them, offering substantial rewards for their courage.

Let me expand on this idea, and I will try to tread carefully to avoid sounding like a guru: The universe is the supplier. It provides the means for everyone who wishes to embark on their journey of self-discovery while respecting their time on Earth. When we give ourselves the chance for the universe to supply, it will. But in modernity, everything has become so mechanized and controlled that we don't even give the universe a fighting chance to enter the room.

We have become so obsessed with metrics, achievement, and reaching our objectives that we want to pave the entire road ahead of us. Ironically, the universe hears our desires and provides exactly what we ask for, laying out the road we demand. But we feel hollow and empty when we reach our destination through the rational mind, the mechanized road. How is this possible? We did not achieve greatness, only an objective. The "check-box mindset" has spoiled the magic of being alive and embracing our creative nature, which is inherently unstructured.

We are not taking advantage of our deep connection with the universe. Instead, we have turned our heads to rational answers. Rare individuals who truly sync with the universe, those who take a leap of faith, can reap the cosmic rewards.

Drawing a line in the sand through introspection can lead to a profound realization. If we find ourselves relentlessly dragging to a job we dislike, merely to "earn a living" without truly feeling alive, we awaken to a deeper truth. This realization signals to the universe that we are ready for change, indicating there's another path ready to be explored.

By acting upon this realization and taking a leap of faith, we effectively direct the universe through *action*—its spoken language—and we become an open channel to communicate with it. This leap of faith doesn't need to be astronomically large. It can be simply taking thirty minutes out of your day to explore the craft you've been deferring for 'someday.' For 'later.'

When I signaled to the universe that I was ready to confront these feelings of emptiness and finally understood that they weren't natural, but rather an indication that I was mechanizing life, serendipity became my norm, not my exception.

I know many might take these ideas as wishful thinking, and you might even believe I'm using these feelings as a defense mechanism to prevent me from realizing I've screwed up my entire career. I cannot prove it with a scientific formula—at least not yet. But I can tell you this: I have never felt as free, as light, as powerful as I do now, and I no longer wear a façade desperately forcing myself to fit into an impossible puzzle. Instead, I have allowed myself the necessary space to see what emerges within me, and it seems that the universe is reciprocating that energy through unexplainable, random situations in my life that just make sense to me. My career, personal life, and creative passions feel totally aligned.

After I made this change, people I had left behind while chasing status suddenly reappeared in the most unexpected and in-your-face ways. I once had a friend who only knew my fake persona. Like a peacock flaunting his tail, I signaled my worth through accomplishments and job titles. I tried to make her like me with these "costly-not-costly" signals, but it had the opposite effect. Acting this way, I never heard back from her.

Months later, I ran into her at a mall. It was a moment packed with serendipity, as if the universe was giving me another chance. I had no job title, no career prospects, and no guard. But that didn't matter. My friend was genuinely happy to see me—not my medals, not my net worth, just me.

That interaction proved to me that the false persona we carry with us to make us feel worthy of other people's respect, love, and attention is just a narrative we tell ourselves. We tell this story because we're too afraid to show ourselves to others in our rawest form, which is just our genuine selves.

Next time you interact with anyone and they ask you what you do at work or in your career, what kind of vehicle you drive to work, or how much you make, try to negate the truth. If you have a job, say you are unemployed; if you drive a Mercedes, say you walk to work; if you make good money, say you are drowned in debt. This exercise will provide two startling truths:

First, it will reveal what the other person really wants from you. Will they want to associate with you for yourself, or just for what you can do for them? It will also help you answer the following questions: Do you want to be with someone who wants you for your persona? Will this relationship flourish naturally, or will it be based on purely "artificial sweeteners?"

Secondly, it will show you that the armor you built around you with your titles, medals, and achievements protected you from a false threat: People worthy of your love will love you for who you are, and they will cherish who you are. You are opening the door for yourself by introducing them to the *real* you.

I had to 'test' this out in a very real way after I quit my job and had to tell people I was unemployed. I always thought people would love me for what I'd accomplished.

Those who stuck with me because of my work status left, and those who *saw me for me* stayed. It was a perfect way to figure out who was interested in what I provided, and my career trajectory, rather than who I was.

Pause and Ponder: Chapter Ten

• Have I truly considered what risk means to me? Not to all the people around me. *Not based on what others have told you, but to you.*

• Have the years just "gone by" for me in a blink of an eye?

• Is time moving much more rapidly as I age?

• Do I want to pursue things for the sake of them but feel hesitant because there is no clear path toward doing so, and the financial penalty could be too high?

• Would any of this matter if I were eighty years old?

• Am I willing to pay the price of never actually risking anything in my life?

• *Try the following exercise: Next time you interact with anyone and they ask you what you do at work or in your career, what kind of vehicle you drive to work, or how much you make, try to negate the truth. Say the exact opposite and watch their reactions, and also pay attention to your own reactions and feelings.*

11

HOW WE ALL CAN NAVIGATE THE GEN Z ECONOMY

Every person must decide at some point, whether they will walk in the light of creative altruism or in the darkness of destructive selfishness.

— *MARTIN LUTHER KING JR.*

In today's society, within our capitalistic system that's ultra-powered—almost on steroids—with technology, we can leverage our tools to build our own path without taking too much of a risk, like quitting our job right away. Pre-existing paths do offer perks, such as stability and certainty, but they fail to reconcile and merge these so-called 'rewards' with purpose and fulfillment.

Unfortunately–or fortunately, depending on how you see it–it seems as though the ideas of predetermined action—following a set path dictated by societal norms—and true purpose and fulfillment are often mutually exclusive. No doubt, if we dare to dive deep into the self, uncertainty and instability will emerge. But rest assured, if we truly commit ourselves to finding and exploring our passions, purpose and fulfillment *will* also emerge.

Modern tools offer the ability to expand the net, seize more opportunities, and open more doors to serendipity without cost. Social media can connect you with people you admire; YouTube can teach you more about your interests; online newsletters can offer a venue to share your ideas and learn new ones independently; a journal can allow you to vent and sort things out; nature can give you space to ask a question and let the answer emerge; friends can lend you an ear. So, rather than jump into the next thing, we can take a step back, knowing that we live in the age of 'Infinite Leverage' with technological tools that can unleash our creative nature, while rewarding us with their compounding, wealth-generating force.

As we have explored previously, sometimes what seems like a step back is actually a step forward.

Capitalism tends to incentivize the *metricalization* of life, prioritizing economic growth and tangible, measurable objectives above everything else, but it gives us creators an unparalleled opportunity to conquer more territory in the playing field as we can leverage our talents at little to no cost; capitalism uniquely incentivizes creativity and innovation by lowering the barriers to entry for creators due to the mechanisms of scale and market accessibility. Take Apple, for instance: the company has invested over $100 billion in iPhone development, yet today, this once-revolutionary device is accessible for as little as $30 a month. The iPhone now serves as a computer, video recorder, audio recorder, finance manager, and a powerful tool for creativity—all within reach of billions of people.[1] Further, it is the only system that "prices in" the luck factor in life–it allows serendipity to flow between creators and creations. This means that even unintended or chance connections between creators and opportunities can result in groundbreaking innovations or products. For instance, a great idea, when paired with the market mechanisms of capitalism, becomes a bridge connecting creators with resources, investors, and audiences from anywhere in the world.

The Gen Z economy and modernized definitions of "work'" and "reward" fueled my long discussions with my late grandfather every time I told him I wanted to switch jobs. Like many of his Baby Boomer comrades, he did not understand how uncommitted I was to my job. Although I had a deep desire to commit to one cause for a long time, deep within me I always felt I was not getting my piece of the pie for the work I produced.

But the looming statistics about the disconnection between productivity, earnings, and access to the coveted American Dream have made me reflect on how hard work, a value I deeply cherish and appreciate, no longer guarantees prosperity. Today, we must embrace a different path toward achieving a new version of the American Dream that disregards the old notions about owning a home, having a stable income, and saving enough for retirement. This new vision embraces the ideal of creative freedom, honoring our time on Earth, and connecting hard work with smart work.

This new vision of the American Dream emerges in the age of Infinite Leverage, a concept coined by Naval Ravikant, where one's efforts can be scaled indefinitely through digital tools and knowledge. He aligns with the idea, thoroughly discussed in this book, that we mistakenly view life as linear, especially in our work: put in eight hours, expect to get back eight hours of output. But it doesn't work that way. Naval emphasizes that what you do, who you do it with, and how you do it are far more important than sheer effort. The quality of your work creates non-linear outputs.

Naval suggests we should work like the king of the jungle. The lion hunts; it doesn't graze like a cow all day. Similarly, we're not meant to graze from nine-to-five; we're meant to hunt. In this new economy, Naval argues, we should function like athletes:

train hard, sprint, rest, reassess. We create a feedback loop, train some more, sprint again, rest, and reassess.

For Naval, the idea that you can achieve linear output by working the same hours every day is for machines. Machines are built for nine-to-five; humans are not.[2]

Again, in a very literal sense, hard work no longer pays off. Few people, only a handful, are reaping most of the rewards and that's because they understand that smart work will always yield more. Rather than focusing on grunt work, they spend resources, such as capital, to acquire a part of a business or found their own. They also embrace the concept of Infinite Leverage.

In this new era of the American Dream powered by infinite leverage, those who create have the upper hand. Those who understand that smart work trumps hard work, that creativity is our true operating software, will build the world.

This new world belongs to the Lion.

Leverage Artificial Intelligence to Unleash Your Creative Nature

The moment you think there aren't any other options is the moment they have won the game. The current way the system is set up provides us with many options. The problem is that few have awakened to this realization, and people often wind up committing themselves to a career that does not fulfill them due to a limited perspective on how to expand their fishing net.

Without a doubt, technology has shifted the momentum from leveraging employers to placing control back in the employee's hands. Current market conditions have shown us that hiring is tough and retaining good employees is tougher. Why? Because employees know they are one click away from changing their whole lives.

Let's start with social media. We are one connection away from building a completely new pathway in our lives. Take LinkedIn (our favorite social media platform to dunk on) as an example. Right now, you can browse a company's staff and their open positions. With just one click, you can connect to the hiring manager, introduce yourself, send your resume and customize a message that expresses your interest in joining them. Do this one hundred times, and one will stick to the board.

Before the internet, employers knew they had the leverage because optionality was out of the question, and companies were built on employee exploitation, paying them the least amount of money legally possible and extracting as much output as they could. Managers' demeanor toward their employees clearly signaled who was in charge. Of course, they're still in charge today, but the leash is stretched and at its weakest point.

With current advancements in AI, the ability to be productive has increased exponentially. In one article, a CEO expressed concern over the possibility that remote employees might be using AI to enhance productivity to such an extent they might be able to work two jobs simultaneously. He also expressed concern when talking about his content writers, who basically use AI to write all their pieces. What was his solution? Rather than adding more incentives for employment retention, such as bonuses for performance or even educating himself on what AI can do for his company, he threatened to 'raise productivity quotas by thirty to fifty times the normal production.'[3]

It is as if corporate America was built with the purpose of maximizing employees suffering rather than productivity. When the old hierarchy rulers sense a drastic change in the social order, they tend to exert every single coercive tool they have. In other words, when they feel threatened, rather than embrace innovation, they try to block it and penalize those who leverage it to enhance their productivity—and consequently, their time on Earth.

James O'Shaughnessy, an investor, writer, founder, and previous guest on my podcast[4] encapsulated this idea brilliantly:

> "One can assume that the old guard will do everything in its power to hang on to their place in the societal hierarchy and it isn't a coincidence to see them spreading and injecting fear, uncertainty and doubt into the discussion about AI, perhaps the most disruptive innovation of my lifetime."[5]

These disruptive technologies enable us to expand optionality. Not only that, they also serve as a truth-revealing tool in terms of the loopholes corporate America has and the real reason people get jobs: to maximize profits.

If the developers who are using AI to work two jobs were happy and found meaning in their first job and money was not part of the equation, they would not find more ways to extract as much money as possible from the system. These kinds of behaviors are the exact reflection of the system: Employers used to extract as much as they could from their employees, and now the employees have the upper hand.

Put differently, this is what a greedy, transactional system gets in return. AI is revealing the truth we all know and have been exploring throughout this writing: We are not working at our jobs for the love of the engagement. Instead, we subconsciously use these newfound technologies as a response to the deeper realization that, if given the chance, we would rather have machines doing our jobs rather than us spending our time on Earth as if we were the machines.

AI is also revealing all the bullshit jobs we don't want to do.

Now, the aftershocks of using these technologies won't give the employees the leverage forever. The CEOs also realize that AI can replace jobs that can be made by actual machines. IBM announced that they will pause all hiring for jobs AI could do, putting more than seven thousand five hundred jobs at risk of being replaced by these technologies. Moreover, a report by Goldman Sachs projected that up to three hundred million jobs could be fully automated using AI.[6]

This means many of us who have allocated most of our focus and time to our careers will have to drastically rethink where we find our purpose in life: What will we do with this newfound time that is not being invested in a job that could have been automated all along? How will people who rely on their jobs cope with unemployment? How will the economy sustain such disruptive movements in the social hierarchy?

During my 2023 interview with Neil deGrasse Tyson, we discussed how Artificial Intelligence has the potential of challenging our identities based on our work, and what would work mean for us now that these machines are on the verge of being able to do them better than us. During our interview, he said:

> "It's inevitable that technology displaces jobs, as it has always done. If jobs are lost and no new ones open up to replace them, then there's a need for some form of universal basic income. Otherwise, people won't have the financial means to purchase the products produced by automation."[7]

I shared with Neil that I was hopeful AI would take over mundane jobs, freeing us from repetitive tasks. This shift could allow us to experience the Overview Effect (discussed in Chapter Eight) from Earth and reflect deeply on our time here, giving us the chance to engage in activities that inspire us. Recently, I had a moment of profound beauty during a walk on a windy day when a rainbow appeared over the ocean. Despite not fully understanding the science behind it, the sight filled me with awe. With AI potentially reducing our work-related preoccupations, we might all have the opportunity to reconnect with our humanity, to step outside and marvel at the simple, miraculous wonders of life—of being alive, like the chance to see more rainbows.

Neil responded by saying this was "a fascinating prediction—one that could be genuinely transformative if it materializes."[8]

Reflecting on the rise of automation in the 1950s and 60s, Neil noted that there was an expectation that the five-day workweek would become obsolete, replaced by a three-day workweek due to machines taking over routine tasks. This shift would allow humans to focus on more complex, value-added work. While the five-day workweek persisted, people could earn five days' worth of income in three days, leaving two days for supplementary income. Looking ahead, Neil suggested that while AI might handle many tasks, certain jobs requiring a human touch, like plumbing, psychology, and social work will remain beyond its capabilities. He added jokingly,

> "AI fixing my plumbing? Not anytime soon. It might be able to diagnose it, but it's not going to come down, bend over with the butt crack showing in the back. Fixing my drain trap? No. There's a human touch and expertise required in tasks that go beyond the capabilities of automation."[9]

I told Neil that one of the things that truly excites me about AI is the prospect of witnessing more artists emerge, more Vincent van Gogh's spurring across the world. We might experience a surge in artistry, creativity, and other avenues to honor our time on Earth. Our creative outputs can become a unique way of connecting with the cosmos itself.

Neil, reflecting on what I said, told me:

> "That's a beautiful way to say it—to honor our time on Earth is to apply our creative mind to everything we do and that we dream of and that we desire. So, it's a brilliant way to think about it. I agree."

But before AI comes for our jobs, before the whole outdated economic system collapses, before we find ourselves trying to find a new identity, and before these technologies can be used for stricter coercion, we can leverage these technologies to build a life of creative freedom, prosperity, and optionality.

Let's say you have a deep passion for politics, you are very informed about how this world works and you have a refined sense of communicating what it is about. Guess what? You've found yourself in the perfect era to translate that passion into a path toward freedom. The tools are at your fingertips—literally. Social media allows you to create quality-driven content that can reach a global audience. By doing so, you may unlock opportunities you never thought possible: connecting with like-minded individuals, forming business partnerships, and even turning your passion into a full-time career.

This is exactly what happened to me. After leaving my full-time job as a speechwriter, I didn't have a clear roadmap, but I knew one thing—I wanted to follow my curiosity, explore conversations that mattered to me, and share them with others.

My podcast, Through Conversations, became a bridge to connect me with some of the most brilliant minds I've long admired–visionaries like Professor Noam Chomsky, Astrophysicist Neil deGrasse Tyson, Evolutionary Psychologist David Buss, Psychoanalyst James Hollis, Neuroscientist Anna Lembke, Astronomer Sara Seager, Philosopher Anil Seth, Sociologist Nicholas Christakis, Philosopher Kieran Setiya, and Neuroscientist Lisa Feldman Barrett, among many others.

Of course, it didn't happen overnight–I've been recording my podcast for five years now–but by consistently recording genuine interviews and sharing my curiosity with the world, the podcast grew into something much larger than I ever anticipated; it gave me a platform to explore ideas, build a community, and foster my creativity.

I'm not alone in this. Consider the founders of Morning Brew, who turned a college newsletter into a thriving business[10], or the creators of theSkimm, who started a simple email digest and grew it into a media empire.[11] In today's asymmetrical economy, we're no longer limited by traditional career paths or the confines of a 9-to-5.

Again, in the age of Infinite Leverage its the quality, the passion–not the grunt work, that offers non-linear outputs.

You just need to start, learn the rules of the game, watch what others are doing in the playground, and start producing. If you don't know how to create a compelling video, I have news for you: AI can do all of this for you. AI software is exploding and the use-cases for it continue to amaze me. You can now use a voice-over AI to narrate your videos, you can ask AI to create videos from scratch, and even ask it to suggest new content for you. Take for example OpenAI's new video generator, Sora, where it creates AI-Generated videos from scratch that are indistinguishable from reality; or xAI that is building the most truthful AI Model that understands the universe.[12]

The ways that AI can help you on your creative path are truly endless. We are now seeing software programs that build an entire website from a doodle drawn on a paper. Grok, xAI's own AI chatbot, can now recognize an image and describe it to you (say you wrote a business plan on a napkin, it can now be processed as a real document); it can help you build your first startup, serving as your digital coach preparing you for your first business pitch; it can also be the source of inspiration for your next big painting. The opportunities are really endless, and as soon as you have finished this chapter, there will be thousands of new ways AI can be used to unlock your creative nature.

I must add just a small caveat here: I would use AI as a starting point and then transition into your own creative vision. You want to get the ball rolling, but try to prevent empowering it to create your content in the long term. At the end of the day, AI-derived content is often without soul—this is our expert domain. This new pathway is based on your passion, and the only way it will feel better than being chained to a cubicle is if it really comes from your heart.

This playing field is an entirely new arena. It is literally uncharted territory with endless possibilities. Our creative nature and potential can be wholly unleashed, and AI can be a powerful tool to unbind the golden handcuffs to which we have chained ourselves.

This is when you must remind yourself that you always have options. The moment they tell you, "This is all you got," and you believe it, that is when you have lost the game. But in today's world, there is always an option out there for you to explore. Once you focus on this, you become dangerous. In the words of Naval, "a taste of freedom can make you unemployable."[13]

Growing Up in the Age of Artificial Intelligence

"Follow your interests, go find what brings you fulfill-ment, and make sure your heart, your passion, and your creative force are aligned with the betterment of society."

— ELON MUSK

In one interview with CNBC, Elon Musk was asked what advice he offers to his kids as we are entering a world in which AI can potentially replace every single job we hold near and dear to our hearts.[14] The exact question was:

"I have kids. One of them will soon go into the workforce. I struggle with how to advise him about a career when technology exists and will only improve. I'm just curious, when you think about advising your children on a career with so much that is changing, what do you tell them that will be of value?"

Elon took a long time to answer, but he began by saying, "Well, it's a tough question to answer."

Yes, Elon, it is perhaps the most difficult question we all must collectively address, as most of us have found meaning through our careers.

Elon continued,

"I guess I would just say, you know, to follow their heart in terms of what they find interesting to do or fulfilling to do and try to be as useful as possible to the rest of society.

If we do get to the sort of magic genie situation where you can ask the AI for anything, and let's say it's even a benign scenario, how do we actually find fulfillment? How do we find meaning in life if the AI could do your job better than you can?

I mean, if I think about it too hard, it can be just dispiriting and demotivating, because I mean, I've put a lot of blood, sweat, and tears into building companies, and then it's like, well, should I be doing this, because if I'm sacrificing time with friends and family that I would prefer to, but then ultimately the AI can do all these things.

Does that make sense? I don't know. To some extent I have to have deliberate suspension of disbelief in order to remain motivated. So, I guess I would say, just you know, work on things that you find interesting, fulfilling, and that contributes some good to the rest of society."

Even to Elon Musk, one of the most influential individuals in the entire world and perhaps our modern age, the challenge that AI poses to humanity's sense of purpose derived from work is one of the most difficult we will ever face. And Elon has put into simple words what I have been trying to express all along: If an AI can do your work for you, and better, would you continue working at your job? Are the blood, sweat, tears and time lost with loved ones worth it?

For Elon, these questions are so deep and truthful he must shut them down to keep his eyes on the ball. Elon ended this segment of the interview with the following sincere reflection:

"Follow your interests, go find what brings you fulfillment, and make sure your heart, your passion, and your creative force are aligned with the betterment of society."

Elon was talking about the cycle of prosperity, optimism, and love we have been discussing along this journey. In a world of rapid automatization and disruptive technologies, the real impact will derive from the activities we pursue that bring us fulfillment. The rest of the jobs will finally be revealed for what they are: bullshit jobs that we made up to keep us in those golden handcuffs. Jobs that give us just enough of an excuse to not pursue what brings us joy. Jobs that keep us from our necessary exploration of our creative selves.

The Serendipitous Search Engine

Before the internet, the big city was the largest generator of happenstance. That magic of pure change that can lead to unimagined opportunity.

Nassim Taleb, an author, scholar, and former trader best known for his work on probability, uncertainty, and risk management, has written a series of bestselling books, including *Fooled by Randomness*, *The Black Swan* and *Antifragile* argues in favor of maximizing our exposure to serendipity. He believes that a big city was the best open-ended place to catch 'as many free non-lottery tickets,' and he was right. In his words:

"Maximize the serendipity around you ... Many people do not realize that they are getting a lucky break in life when they get it. If a big publisher (or a big art dealer or a movie executive or a hotshot banker or a big thinker) suggests an appointment, cancel anything you have planned: you may never see such a window open up again. I am sometimes shocked at how little people realize that these opportunities do not grow on trees. Collect as many free non lottery tickets (those with open-ended payoffs) as you can, and, once they start paying off, do not discard them. Work hard, not in grunt work, but in chasing such opportunities and maximizing exposure to them. This makes living in big cities invaluable because you increase the odds of serendipitous encounters—you gain exposure to the envelope of serendipity."[15]

Nassim Taleb and Naval Ravikant, both thinkers that have influenced the way I see the world, agree on the importance of maximizing serendipity. They also seem to be aligned with the idea that we should pursue activities that have no ceiling in terms of upside, but offer a limited downside. In other words, we must expand our range field, our fishing net, if you will, as much as possible to attract and catch as many asymmetrical opportunities as possible. This allows life to reveal all its hidden treasures. There are plenty of ways to amplify our serendipity field, but Naval offers a few that allow us to tap into the power of leverage and provide our access into what I refer to as the Asymmetrical Economy:

Asymmetric Opportunities by Naval:[16]

• Invest in startups

• Start a company

• Create a book, podcast, or video

• Create a (software) product

• Go on many first dates

- Go to a cocktail party

- Read a Lindy Book

- Move to a big city

- Buy Bitcoin

- Tweet

This is a comprehensive list of activities we should pursue to lure the goddess of opportunity into our lives. Going on many first dates might seem emotionally tolling, but the upside is you potentially find a life partner. The downside is investing an hour getting to know a stranger and having a keen interest in them, while navigating the butterflies we feel in our stomach with each encounter. It's the best of all worlds; going to a cocktail party is also a great way to expand our fishing net, as we allow ourselves an opportunity to interact with individuals from all spheres of life, given that they are all clustered in one space at the same time.

As Nassim Taleb puts it in *Black Swan*,

> "You can't even start to know what you may find on the envelope of serendipity. If you suffer from agoraphobia, send colleagues."[17]

I love that, you'll never know what you'll find on the envelope of serendipity.

Investing in a startup or starting your own company is also a powerful asymmetrical opportunity. Given that our true nature as human beings seeks to *create*, to build, and to be a force of creativity, there's no more impactful statement we can make to the universe that we are ready to receive its gifts than to start our own project.

When we start our own company, we create an offering for the world's canvas embedded with our creative powers. And when we invest in a startup or in someone else's "moonshot vision," we empower the founders to build their own castle, hoping that, in return, we reap the rewards of their creative efforts with them.

This is also true of writing a book, starting a podcast, or posting on X (formerly Twitter). When I started Through Conversations, I had no idea it would evolve into a platform connecting me with some of the brightest minds of our time. It began as a simple passion project, requiring little more than curiosity, a microphone, and the courage to reach out to people I admired, and it has profoundly enriched my own creative journey. I also want to add that my podcast has become even stronger than my curriculum when it comes to pursuing new career paths. For example, I landed my first job ever because of the podcast—not because of my curriculum. In fact, I've had more opportunities open up for me because of the podcast than any credential on my résumé. That's another externality of following your passion: you never know what doors may open for you when you embrace the serendipitous path.

As mentioned, we are but one click away from connecting with like-minded individuals. Alternatively, the cost of starting a blog is virtually nonexistent, and the upside is endless; recording a podcast has essentially no entry barriers and provides unlimited opportunities to connect with other like-minded people. Writing a post costs one hundred forty characters, but it can become a book or a business.

In modernity, creativity is a precondition of and necessarily works in conjunction with asymmetric opportunities, leveraging gains and amassing income. Whereas big cities used to be hubs for professional/social interaction and creative inspiration, the internet has superseded it as the decisive catalyst for such exchanges.

We must lure the goddess of opportunity to us. In modernity, that goddess is a colossal web of information, literally at our fingertips. And with a click of a button, we can engage with anyone in the world. Therefore, our tiny yet massive blue marble floating in space has become smaller than ever.

Today, the new big city is the internet.

We can feed this machine with our creative output and see how it impacts the world. We can use the internet as a powerful serendipitous tool to leverage our social connectivity and increase our exposure to asymmetrical opportunities. Some experts theorize that we are all just six degrees of separation away from each other, and the internet bears out the theory more than ever.

During Stanley Milgram's 1967 "Small World Problem" experiment, random people were tasked with passing information between another random person through a chain of people they knew. Milgram found that the average chain was 5.5 people long. His findings were so powerful, they motivated the creation of many websites (such as Facebook) that leveraged the internet to connect with anyone we want in the world.[18]

These platforms also tested the validity of the theory. In 2001, Duncan Watts, a professor at Columbia University, repeated Milgram's experiment using e-mail. He sent a message to forty-eight thousand people, and they had to forward it to someone they knew whom they recognized to be one step closer to the target person Watts wanted to reach. Again, Watts found that the average number of intermediaries was around six.[19]

In 2011, a group of Microsoft researchers reviewed more than thirty billion messages and found that the average number of degrees of separation between any two people was 6.6.[20]

The six-degrees-of-separation theory can motivate us to pursue our creative passions to build a bridge between us and our dream life. What if we were all six degrees away from a connection that would facilitate our dream life?

The risk of sharing our creative passions has never had so much upside with so little downside than right now.

If this book hasn't convinced you that life isn't just about maximizing payoffs, there's one area where you should focus on maximizing: seeking serendipity. Test the six degrees of separation theory, not just socially, but also in ways that enhance your creative nature. Use the internet as the serendipitous search engine that it is.

As Albert Einstein said, "Creativity is contagious: Pass it on..."

Final Thoughts on the New Gen Z Economy

The Asymmetric Economy offers us a way to *leverage* leverage. That is, asymmetrical opportunities are a unique ticket to harnessing the power of the universe to create magic in our lives. They're the closest we have to a magic wand, but even better because they must include our efforts, passion, and creativity. In other words, *we* are the main characters creating the magic. We are the key pieces of the puzzle that makes it all happen and connect. These asymmetric opportunities enable us to become individuals with an unlimited sense of agency while also giving space for serendipity to enter the room. As with all meaningful things in life, it must start with us.

While our efforts will certainly not *always* pay off and some of these asymmetric opportunities may not come to fruition, they also allow us, as Nassim Taleb notes, to "wear your best for your execution." They allow us to show our best colors and stand dignified with our efforts. It's less about the outcome, and more about our commitment to exploring these asymmetric opportunities.[21]

It's no secret that we live in a chaotic, random world. But if we subscribe to the Gen Z Economy, we stand a great chance to harness the power of randomness, while giving it its merited respect, and make it work in our favor. Given that we cannot control outcomes, we must always remember that how we react is always in our control. As Taleb puts it,

> "Your last recourse against randomness is how you act—if you can't control outcomes, you can control the elegance of your behavior. You will always have the last word."[22]

It is also important to note that within the Gen Z Economy, we must be cautious about the energy we put in. You can't just say, "I want luck to follow my efforts" while having a cynical attitude. Furthermore, when we punch our ticket into this new economy, we must also be wary of who joins the ride with us. In other words, optimism, positivity, and effort are in while cynicism, negativity, and slothfulness are out. While it is true that our actions are the best signals of our efforts, our attitude is a precondition to everything. Actions and attitude always go hand in hand.

Think of it like baking a cake: you need both the right ingredients and the correct technique. Just as you can't bake a perfect cake with only the ingredients or only the technique, you can't achieve success with just the right actions or the right attitude alone. Both are essential and inseparable. As Taleb wisely observes,

> "Avoid losers. If you hear someone use the words 'impossible', 'never', or 'too difficult' too often, drop him or her from your social network. Never take 'no' for an answer (conversely, take most 'yeses' as 'most probably')."

Drop the losers, bring in the winners.

It is also essential to understand that hard work will only get you so far. While we should always give it our all, we must remain unattached to the outcome. As Victor Levy, author of *Life is Setting Me Up for Success* and previous guest on my podcast[23] says, we must always be

> "fully committed, completely unattached."[24]

We must do our best to send a strong signal to the serendipitous goddess that we are worthy of what's inside her envelope, but it will remain true forever that our efforts won't always bear fruit. We need luck in our lives, but we can only control our commitment to our craft, not the outcomes of it. As much as I want to believe that hard work is the secret recipe to solve all our problems, we also need luck. Still, the more we strike two rocks together, the greater the likelihood of igniting a spark that lights up a fire.

Pause and Ponder: Chapter Eleven

• How can you increase your range of serendipity?

• What opportunities does your heart lean towards in this new Asymmetrical Economy?

• What is one step you can take to leverage Artificial Intelligence for your creative passions?

• Write down six potential degrees of separation between you and your dream life. Try to connect the dots but don't hold on too tightly to them.

12

BUILD YOUR OWN PARIS

It is so, my dear Lucilius; there are a few men whom slavery holds fast, but there are many more who hold fast to slavery.

SENECA, LETTER XXII

"I want to feel things in life, April," Frank declared. "Really, feel them. How's that for an ambition?"

Set in the late 1950s, Revolutionary Road[1] follows Frank and April Wheeler, a suburban couple grappling with the monotony of their lives. Once full of ambition and dreams, they now find themselves trapped in a cycle of unfulfilling routines. After rediscovering a photograph of Frank in Paris, April envisions a daring escape: selling their possessions and moving to Paris to rekindle their love and passions. "You'll have time to figure out what you actually want to do," April says, urging Frank to take the leap. This would allow Frank to tap into his creative passions while April carried the heavy load and went to work. Paris was the only city Frank looked forward to visiting again, and the young couple could begin with a clean slate.

The idea appeared bold and, as Frank initially observed, "unrealistic," to which April replied,

"No, Frank, this is what's unrealistic: It's unrealistic for a man with a fine mind to go on working year after year at a job he can't stand, coming home to a place he can't stand, to a wife who's equally unable to stand the same things."

But when Frank is offered a lucrative promotion and April learns she is pregnant, their resolve is tested. Frank retreats into the safety of conformity, while April, devastated by their unraveling dreams, takes drastic measures, leading to a tragic conclusion.

The Wheeler's story tells us that when we find the courage to take a leap of faith according to our hearts desire, life sends unforeseen challenges to test our resolve, courage, and the *worthiness* of that pursuit. These situations pose as solutions, which often include a lucrative job offer that serves as a "lifeline" so we don't take that leap of faith. However, in reality, that offer may be a death sentence.

A leap of faith is the ultimate revolutionary step we can choose in our lives. And while it may seem that life is giving us an "out" from our dreams or a better offer—whether a new job or a friend's cautionary tale or the birth of a child—these are stress tests of our courage and resolve. In other words, if we truly reflect on the situations that arise between the act of making our decision to take that leap of faith and realizing the dream, the game completely shifts in our favor. We no longer see the improved job offer as a savior but as a test of our resolve, and what our close circle tells us about "our childish dreams" becomes a glaring indicator that we are onto something.

These *"savior-esque"* situations often appeal to our rational mind more than our intuitive spirit.

Still, while it is hard to accept, some people cannot envision living without a leash, and when challenges suddenly arise—such as an unexpected financial obligation or the security of a high-paying job offer—they often serve as convenient excuses to retreat from pursuing their dreams. For instance, someone might abandon their plan to start a startup after receiving an enticing corporate promotion, or delay their creative aspirations because of mounting student loan payments. These moments, while seemingly practical, often tether individuals further to a life they don't truly want.

However, these "problems" are in fact opportunities. And this can only be true if—and only if—we embark on a sincere leap of faith. And, surely, every one of us must take our unique, personalized contexts into account. But my impression about life is that, when we follow our heart, when we follow our true desires, everything aligns the way it should.

Granted, the bumps in the road will never be pleasant. The challenges thrown at Frank and April were indeed frightening. But why did Paris and the pursuit of their dream suddenly seemed untenable, impossible? What was their worst-case scenario? If Paris had not worked out, and it was absolutely impossible to raise their child in a new country, it's not as if they could not come back to their old lives, with the added value of all their experiences while living abroad for a period of their lives.

In the real world, people like Amanda Hesser, co-founder of Food52, face similar crossroads. With twin babies to care for, she could have easily succumbed to the fear of uncertainty. Instead, she used all her savings to launch her startup, knowing that failure was a possibility but choosing to take the leap anyway.[2]

Sometimes the fear of failure blinds us to the resilience and adaptability we inherently possess.

Sometimes we use "problems" as a convenient excuse to abandon our dreams, much like the Wheelers' did with their unborn baby.

Take Markus Persson, the creator of Minecraft, who faced a similar crossroads in his personal life. While working a regular programming job and juggling the pressures of family life, including the birth of his child, Markus could have easily used his responsibilities as a reason to avoid pursuing his passion for independent game development. Instead, he took a leap of faith, dedicating himself to creating Minecraft in his spare time. The game not only became a monumental success but also revolutionized the video game industry.[3]

Reflecting on the worst-case scenario of decision-making can be a powerful fear-setting exercise. It allows us to reset our imaginary, often ridiculous 'death sentences' and enables us to see a path of opportunity with much more clarity. Tim Ferriss, in his blog post on "fear-setting," explains how this exercise helps people face their fears by clearly defining them and their potential consequences. He suggests visualizing the worst-case scenario and listing ways to mitigate it, which often reveals that the feared outcomes are manageable and less catastrophic than imagined. In his words:

"Conquering Fear = Defining Fear"[4]

But what about another important exercise: *love-setting?* If we follow our hearts, what could be in store for us? If we choose our lives based on worst-case-scenario prevention in every respect, will we miss out on what life has to offer—the endless opportunities that could potentially be forthcoming.

It seems to me that the way we have been programmed—either evolutionarily or societally or a combination of both, we're better suited to envision a life of fear prevention rather than fear removal. That is, we are hard-wired to mentally predetermine how the linear path will unfold than to carve out an unknown path in Paris, for example, where our dreams take precedence and surprising twists and turns in the road will rise to meet us.

When we envision our lives in our modern times, we clearly see the linear path as well: We graduate, get a job, get married and have kids, and we do what we must to squeeze as many life-moments as we can within each milestone. But when we begin to imagine a new path—one that is not conventional and makes our hearts race, we can't really linearize it within our minds, and it is almost impossible to see where it could lead. And we have been programmed (again, maybe because it helped us survive) to shy away from paths that cannot be imagined.

We are inherently limitless with a limited mindset—a contradiction that we must resolve by choice. In a way, we find life when we cross that unimaginable path. We are perhaps living in the most inviting moment in human history to take a leap of faith and give life a chance to guide us steer the way, following our creative nature—or at least allowing time for it to emerge.

Most of our fears in today's world are but figments of our imagination. Tribes do not hunt us; we are not prey to lions in the wilderness; we are not merely existing or living just to survive—we can build a life to thrive. So, perhaps we can realize, once and for all, that we can live to realize our creative potential and embark on our own Revolutionary Road.

The Time Is Now to take advantage of our historically unprecedented opportunities for prosperity and take a leap of faith—give life a chance to guide us as we try to find our own Paris—whatever we define that to be.

We should see Frank and April's story as a cautionary tale of backing out from our leap of faith. I once met a talented graphic designer who spent years working at a job she despised because she was too afraid of the uncertainty that came with freelancing. She dreamed of starting her own design studio, but the thought of losing the "stability" of her paycheck kept her anchored to her desk. Over time, her passion waned, and she grew increasingly resentful, stuck in a cycle of self-doubt. It wasn't until her company downsized, forcing her into the freelance world, that she discovered she could thrive independently and reignite her love for design.

As I write these words, while recognizing the rewards of pursuing my creative passions and allowing my true self to emerge, the temptation to return to the linear path seems only to increase in magnitude. The reason: I have received multiple job offers with the salary, access, and prestige no sane person would refuse, and the pushback from my network seems to escalate all the time. They often saw me as childish and immature—a rebel without a cause. But I don't hold it against them. Instead, I see these situations as stress tests of my creative resolve. And, yes, I may be a rebel without a cause, and that, in itself, is my cause: to let my creative nature come to light and express itself organically–to let my path express itself naturally.

In other words, I'm building my own "Paris."

As you embark on your creative journey, I wish you nothing but strength, resolve, and courage. While we are not being chased by wild boars—or chimpanzees, for that matter, that does not mean the challenges we face are simple: the temptations to stick to a linear path are almost irresistible.

Although there are many people out there that have taken their leap of faith, they are still the minority—and the economic as well as the social toll we could face are not imaginary; they have a real power to disrupt our lives.

But all that pales in comparison to what we could become when we imagine the unimaginable and pursue the non-pursuable. I wish you the time and patience to allow yourself to grow into someone you never imagined you could become although you always knew, deep within you, you could become.

Now go find—go build—your own Paris.

Keep Your Cards Close to Your Chest

For most of us, our first impulse when something good, something aligned with our hearts happens, is to share the big news with our circle.

When we share our dreams with friends or acquaintances, they might project their own doubts and insecurities onto us. They often disguise their advice as the wisdom they would want if they were in our position.

Remember that the brighter a light shines, the longer the shadow it casts.

When we open ourselves to critical judgment and the grip of societal norms and expectations tightens around us, the parts of our careers that speak to our heart are impacted.

Often, those who challenge the status quo present themselves (at least to those who operate solely within the lines) as insane. Often, those who challenge the status quo are seen as unconventional, even insane, by those who cling to the norm. Take Elon Musk, for example. Before Tesla became a household name, his vision of making electric vehicles mainstream was widely mocked. Critics labeled him as overly ambitious, even delusional, for challenging the automotive industry. Yet, Musk pursued this dream with relentless determination, fundamentally reshaping the landscape of sustainable transportation.

What a profound message. In today's world, the decision to be relentless, driven, and live a life as if it matters is often mistaken for insanity. But fading away at a meaningless job for forty years straight is shockingly *not* irrational. That, my friends, is wrongly perceived as being smart, rational, and mature. That is the "definition" of a *modern* person.

But what is the real definition of living authentically? Is complying with what society expects from us, which includes paying a mortgage, being indebted to our necks, not being expressive, and explosive—chaotic, even—living authentically? Or is it giving ourselves the time and space to reflect on what would make our lives more meaningful, regardless of societal expectations?

An authentic individual leads a life he wants, not the life society expects of him.

I want to embrace that definition of an individual.

I want to lead a life that I—and only I—want.

Living authentically means leading a life that aligns with your true desires, not the life others expect of you.

It's about embracing the freedom to define your own path and living a life that you—and only you—truly want.

Again, life throws stress tests at us. They are intentional challenges life presents as we take our leap of faith to discover what we're truly made of. Most people give in to the allure of deceptive opportunities because they seem too tempting to refuse. For some, the allure of a high-paying job that could provide for their growing family, coupled with their own fear and insecurities, can widen the cracks in their determination. For others, questions about raising a baby in an entirely different country without financial stability, and the opinions of others, flood their minds. The doubts multiply, and they begin to choose what seems rational over what feels right. Over what other people believe is better for them. Naval once said that,

"If you want to make the wrong decision, ask everyone."[5]

Reflecting on personal experiences, I, too, have encountered similar situations. When I quit my job and my boss praised my last piece of work for the first time ever, was that praise the beginning of a fun turn in my job? Should I have stayed to find out, even though I was becoming miserable?

When I finally left my work to pursue my creative passions, I was presented with multiple "you-can't-refuse" types of offers—opportunities promising a high salary, prestige, and a vast network. People close to me began to chirp in my ear on what they thought was the best course of action for me, and I listened. But beneath the surface of such enticing offers lies the potential to extinguish our cherished aspirations. Life tests our commitment to exploring our truth, honoring our time on Earth, and pursuing our creative passions.

Remember: When the light shines brightly, the shadow cast is longer.

This means that when we set our intentions to become who we need to be, the challenges will become greater—the grip of the Matrix becomes tighter. This happens across many areas of our lives, not just careers.

But let us believe that life hands us these situations to test our visions, our intentions, and frankly, our worthiness to realize our potential—our potential as partners, our potential as fully integrated individuals, our potential as creative forces of nature, our agency in choosing to live life as if it matters. These obstacles don't mean we shouldn't take a leap of faith. They're just meant to fortify ourselves as we do.

Pause and Ponder: Chapter Twelve

• What is your own Paris? How can you start building it?

• What is one place in the world that makes you really feel things in life? When was the last time you visited?

• What bold dreams remain inside your soul but continue to defer to the future? When you think about making this dream come true, what happens in your body? What if you leaned towards these feelings?

• Are there any "imaginary problems" you have created that stop you from unleashing your creative potential?

• Write down the names of three people who are close to you and you'd know they would never discourage you from taking a leap of faith. Make sure you only trust them and their advice along your self-discovery journey.

13

THE LIFE PRINCIPLES OF VIA NEGATIVA

One does not accumulate but eliminate. It is not daily increase but daily decrease. The height of cultivation always runs to simplicity.

— BRUCE LEE

Less is more.

Nassim Taleb's work concerns problems of randomness, probability, and uncertainty. He embraced the concept of *Via Negativa* (Latin for "the Negative Way") to make better life decisions. The term derives from apophatic theology, which was intended to describe God by what he is not, rather than what he is.

According to Taleb, *Via Negativa* involves subtracting or eliminating elements or factors from our lives rather than actively trying to add or achieve positive outcomes.[1]

Taleb argues that when we have limited knowledge or understanding of the complex systems or processes at play, *Via Negativa* allows us to minimize risk and uncertainty by focusing on what we can control. He also suggests that this approach can help us to avoid the pitfalls of over-confidence and hubris, which can lead us to take unnecessary actions in pursuit of our objectives.

We can apply this concept, heavily used in investing, risk management, and finances, to honor our time on Earth. *Via Negativa* is all about removing the stuff and fluff; the illusory responsibilities we have acquired that, in fact, have acquired us. It's all about pausing the grandiose life plan we have built for ourselves and evaluate what we own, and what owns us.

More often than not, while it may be difficult to realize, our possessions *possess* us. More often than not, we don't own our dreams—our dreams *own* us. More often than not, we don't possess our ideologies—our ideologies *possess* us.

When blind competition towards the pursuit of acquisition and accumulation drives our society, life becomes superficial and trivial. There is an alternative. We can collaborate, build on each other's ideas, and do away with self-congratulation and envy. We can begin to wear new identities based on compassion, trust, and integrity instead of the have-or-have-not mindset. By doing this, we start to live—not merely exist. We no longer see people as means to an end–coworkers as just pawns to achieve a promotion, supervisors as just gatekeepers to raises, and networking just reduced to transactional exchanges; we also no longer treat our time as a waste but as our most cherished asset. Consequently, we start appreciating other people's time and inherent value—their *being*.

As our collective consciousness expands, we become cosmically aware of how precious our life is, and we instantly appreciate the infinite value and purpose of others—the assets of time, family, and community.

Paradoxically, as we strip away the trivialities in life, we come to realize the vast wealth we already possess.

The crazy aspect of our search for monetary wealth is the difficulty in reaching it—today more than ever. At the time of writing in 2024, wages have stagnated, the cost of living keeps rising, access to affordable education is virtually nonexistent, and owning a home is a distant dream only our parents could enjoy.[2]

We have reached a point where we normalize this way of living at the expense of our own selves; it is customary to work at a job we hate just to make ends meet; it is normal to pay off our student loans for twenty years; meeting people through dating apps and seeing others as a 'gamified' experience is normal because we don't have the time or energy to interact in person.

The endless, insane quest for success fractures our sense of community; we have never been as alienated as we are today from our neighbors. When was the last time you invited a neighbor to your home, or a neighbor asked you to theirs? If you live in a condominium, do you know the names of the occupants who share the same floor? Have you ever even seen their faces?

We are so caught up in this meaningless chase that our systems and ways of living have reflected that to us: We are an atomized society that values material riches over real wealth.

A society entangled in wealth-quest insanity operates as follows:

• Many are caught up in a job for almost ten hours a day—with an hour-long commute both ways.

• Many compete for a promotion that promises even more money and prestige.

• People argue with each other through digital platforms and say things they would never dare to do in person, so they don't build relationships and continue to focus on the senseless wealth-quest.

• People feel animosity toward each other when they see each other in person because they are a direct threat to their pursuit of freedom, wealth, and the broken definition of the American Dream–if someone else succeeds, it might come at their expense.

We are socialized to pursue excess, incentivized to consume, spend, and accumulate as much as possible. For example, do a house check and take an inventory of the products you purchased in the last year but have used less than three times. You will be surprised: that outfit you desperately needed but used just for one night; those shoes that were on sale, practically calling out to you, "buy me or you'll regret it!" Why did you need them?

We get an astonishing visual when we think about the accumulation of products and our excesses. Almost everyone in a capitalistic system can relate to buying things we don't need. But this phenomenon doesn't just affect our consumer behaviors; it permeates our entire life. For parents, this may translate into working tirelessly to provide an overflow of toys, gadgets, and clothes for their children—many of which hold little lasting value. But does this sacrifice of time, energy, and happiness truly serve the family's well-being?

Think about your career. Maybe you've landed your "dream job" that pays a hefty salary, has a good upside for promotions, and earns you peer recognition and respect. Eventually, however, you realize how strenuous it has become to keep up with your "dream job," and it is making you feel drained—a great indicator that your job is not your calling. Worse, the job has snatched you away from what you love doing and your creative passions, and has put itself between you and your loved ones. Then, you begin to sacrifice your time for your "dream job." In other words, you don't own what you thought of as your dream. Instead, your deceptive illusion owns you.

Put differently, what you measure as success, wealth, prestige, and power, begins to measure you. Paul Portesi, a brilliant thinker who shares his ideas through X, eloquently writes,

> "Observe how you measure people: by intelligence, weight, height, status, politics... What you measure measures you. You are measured by what you measure. It indicates what you're emotionally attached to. Careful of the observable measurable. People will try to optimize that."[3]

This is a very powerful message: *You become measured by what you measure.* Let that sink in. You were once chasing that product, that net worth, that job, but long before you knew it, these began to chase you. It becomes a self-fulfilling cycle—an endless chase just to keep you going—an obsession with hoarding more—only to ultimately never own anything.

 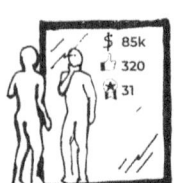

Deep within you, you start feeling a sense of emptiness, disappointment, and rage. You have been told all your life that wealth would equal freedom. But look at the reality: It has never been harder to own a home or to enjoy a quality education without becoming indebted for life to predatory institutions, and most of all, to be truly free.

Side note—if you were wondering, yes, as the book is coming to an end, I am indeed trying to light a fire under your ass until you feel like you're boiling with the desire to honor your time on Earth through your own conventions.

Society has become obsessed with measuring success through observable metrics (i.e., wealth, career, awards), and obsessive measurement can be more harmful than beneficial. That is why adopting a philosophy based on growing by removing, rather than growing by *growing*, is the perfect way to find our path on Earth —the *Via Negativa* way. The art of removal.

When we remove all our labels, our identity based on what we do, what we own, and how much we're worth, we can begin our real search. The search for our own path.

After all these years, have you ever allocated time to stop, to take a sabbatical, to remove rather than add and reflect, or is that time reserved for when you retire? If you have been playing an artificially modern game forever, that game starts playing you— meaning you have transformed into a completely new character built to work rather than to live. Doing something averse to our inclinations, such as working at a job we hate, changes our brain's neural connections and *literally* makes us a different person.

Well, on second thought, in some cases, that might not be entirely bad. Becoming someone altogether different with a new identity due to the stress of work and tying up life's purpose with a career may be a good thing for some, as it eliminates the responsibility— the *real challenge of removing the mask—to discover one's true identity.*

If you want to subscribe to this idea, just remember that you might pay a hefty price to play that game. Will this game compel you to surrender yourself? If so, you might experience a serious detriment.

Again, what we measure, measures us. What we work on, works on us. What we put our time into, puts time on us. If we work ourselves to death, we do so because we believe in the false promise everyone clings to: "Upon retirement, all this hard work will pay off. I will finally reap the rewards of my pension benefits, prestige, and wealth, and I will be able to enjoy what I loved doing before sacrificing years of my life, forfeiting the pursuit of my dreams. Deferring pleasure and the pursuit of true callings is just how the system works, I guess."

Well, that system is playing you. The game you played, *played you*.

If the prevailing evidence proved the contrary, and more people felt connected to their jobs, possessions, wealth, and how they spent their time on this planet, this book would never exist. But, no doubt, we're doing something wrong.

We can experiment by employing new ways of living to figure out what works. Living life *Via Negativa* can help us find that path, and we will witness a new opportunity unfold. It's called freedom.

But freedom requires courage. Scratch that. It requires out-of-this-world levels of courage. Freedom *Via Negativa*-style doesn't guarantee anything but *less*—less of what you have been told life should be all about, to allow life to grow into what it truly is.

Too many people battle to get that promotion, own that big ticket item, and impress that person. Those who see through this sense-less, worldly game have a distinct advantage: the decision to exit and build their own life trajectory. Too many people live according to the philosophy, "accumulate today, enjoy later." Too many live under the illusory spell of "wealth through accumulation."

Become the exception.

Finding True Purpose and Meaning

The less you have, the more you own.

On our true path to finding purpose and meaning, we must culti-vate our creative spirits and uplift others. Only then can we begin to amass genuine, enduring wealth.

Don't get me wrong. I'm not advocating for a World-Economic-Forum dystopian version of reality where no one owns anything, and our food is produced in synthetic laboratories. Instead, I hope to open your eyes to your life, your self-worth, and your sense of purpose as a function of how much you already own, how much you have already achieved, how much you're already worth, and to embrace an entirely new approach to living, fashioned by a *Via-Negativa* consciousness. You have arrived at your billionaire-status destination now, just think about how much time you still have on Earth; with those around you and with yourself.

I believe that you are a reader of great imagination: So, imagine all of us would live in a reality where we build our career around our life rather than build our life around our career. Our whole paradigm would shift, and true purpose emerge. Careers worth sacrificing for are built; communities of optimistic people are formed, and relationships based on the better angels of our nature are organically created.

We can start to build this reality by first taking a step back and asking ourselves, "Why do I have a need to accumulate in the first place?" Such inner self-exploration allows us to understand the meaning of being alive and our true motivations as we navigate life, including our evolutionary blueprint, self-awareness, societal norms, and the human condition.

If only my eighteen-year-old self could have accessed and truly understood these principles, I never would have chosen to be lonely on the journey; I never would have chosen to feel disconnected from society; I never would have chosen to feel like a pawn; I never would have chosen maximizing success over finding long-lasting meaning in my life.

As a society, we too can ask ourselves these questions from a macro-scale perspective:

• Do we want to sacrifice overall happiness to increase our GDP? (Are these mutually exclusive?)

• Do we really want to track every aspect of our lives to optimize our time on Earth, improving irrelevant, abstract metrics while looking the other way and failing to face our challenges?

• Do we really want to chase high-prestige jobs in exchange for our true selves?

• Do we really want to take orders all our lives from lost people who caught themselves inside the Matrix and now want to entrap us, too?

• Do we really want to sacrifice the prime of our lives to save enough money for retirement instead of enjoying the things that already make us happy?

I believe that by exploring these questions, we regain a sense of self, purpose, and meaning and re-construct the fabric of society. Many of us are fed a daily dose of the importance of *hustling*, working all day, and seeing people on social media earning millions and sharing their crazy lifestyles. We have not asked ourselves why we are compelled to share such information on social media; we have not asked ourselves what true virtuosity is; instead, we see what society wants us to see and often believe it at face value.

In a world driven by algorithms and likes, many of us confuse the curated versions of success and happiness we see on social media with reality. This disconnect can erode our ability to experience love, bonding, and fulfillment in their deepest forms. Studies have shown that social media often amplifies feelings of inadequacy and disconnection, as our brains struggle to distinguish between the fiction of a one-minute reel and the complexity of real life.[4]

This is where Via Negativa comes into play: by removing what doesn't matter—the incessant need for external validation and superficial comparisons—we make space to reconnect with what truly does, like purpose, authentic relationships, and our own definition of success.

When we focus on living deeply and intentionally, we see that real success inspires us to lift others up, not to commodify them for personal gain. True fulfillment comes not from flaunting a curated life but from engaging fully with the messiness and richness of reality. By removing these distractions, we can better focus on what it means to live authentically and meaningfully.

By embracing the principles of *Via Negativa*, we can redefine who we are, how we love, and what we invest our most precious asset on from a first-principle approach, one that can guarantee we look ourselves into a mirror that reflects our truest, rawest, *most sincere self.*

Then, when we are butt-naked staring into the abyss of our souls, we can create a bottom-up (see what I did there?) system that energizes our creative nature.

Thinking About Our Life in Charts

> The superior man acts before he speaks, and afterwards speaks according to his action.

These pages have revealed that I used to be a fan of optimizing my life through career achievement, recognition, and the external metrics of success, such as wealth, job titles, and experience. Since my perspective has changed, I now honor my time on Earth by tuning into my intuition, creative spirit, and passions. One metric-driven exercise helped me realize how I was wasting my time on this tiny yet massive blue marble.

When I was sucked into living my life through my job, I became aware of how much time I was spending on commutes, office politics, and wearing a mask rather than investing my time in what fulfilled me. As discussed extensively throughout this book, this trade-off between passion and work has been the norm for over a century and has killed more dreams than any other virus.

As young individuals, my peers, colleagues, and I look to older generations for wisdom and ask them, "How should I spend my twenties?" or "When is the right time to pursue our dreams?" and the most common answer almost always is, "First, you need to save enough money so you can later enjoy doing what you love to do, but before that, you should keep your head down, follow instructions, and earn a decent living."

Whether you're in your twenties, forties, or sixties, it's easy to get trapped in this cycle–but when we actually look at it for what it is, we can change course.

We live our lives in charts. We track our progress, our health, our finances, our relationships; we use charts to make decisions, set goals, and measure our success. It seems as though our end-goal is to optimize every single aspect of our lives, obsessing over making progress. As we have explored throughout this book, optimization should be left for robots and Artificial Intelligence, and we should focus on embracing and exploring our creative nature. But what if we think about our lives in charts differently? What if we could leverage the power of charts to help us understand ourselves better, make better choices, and live more fulfilling lives?

An especially critical point here—and expressed many times throughout this book—is that any given career objective or undertaking must *not* carry a negative connotation. The central issue is that we should align ourselves with who we are and want to become. Any path that emerges from our true selves, and enables us to tap into our true identity—be it work, a relationship, or a creative pursuit—has deeply inherent value.

In earlier chapters, I described how my last job left me feeling depleted, and some tasks felt like control rather than actual work. But I must stress one point: if the job would have been aligned with my core, any task presented to me, however mundane and meaningless, would still have been thought of as meaningful, in and of itself.

In other words, work is not an inherently negative aspect of our lives. I hope that this book will inspire you to open yourself up to the possibility of finding a career, a relationship, with others as well as with yourself, or a creative pursuit that honors your time on Earth and allows you to explore your creative potential.

When I envisioned investing my time in terms of a bar chart, each bar reflected a different area of my life—my career, relationships, community, creativity, and so on. But I saw just one massive bar I cultivated: work.

I realized then that the more I waited to water the seeds of what actually makes me human, the less opportunity they had to sprout. And the more time I continued putting all my eggs in the success basket, I would risk losing my creative force of nature.

So, I drew two different bar charts: one that faced reality—that is, how I am actually investing my time on Earth—and one I wished were real—that is, how my ideal time allocation would manifest.

The present bar chart showed how much time I was spending on things that didn't necessarily speak to my heart (my career, my resource accumulation, my reputation) and how little attention I paid to my creativity, my community, and my relationships.

Don't get me wrong: I still managed to pursue creative endeavors, involve myself with my community, and go on many dates. Although I was working on my own podcast, I felt as if I was just going through the motions—just like Ram Dass, I played the game but was not part of the game. Although I was involved in my community, I never really felt part of it, and although I dated while I was working, I never felt present with the other person.

That being said, in my ideal bar chart, I envisioned myself being truly intentional with my time allocation, and the whole visual changed: My career shrank by a ton, my creative pursuits grew exponentially, my community involvement was enormous, and my relationships were finally nurtured.

Here is the key word: 'intentional.' This newfound time is not about just checking a box; it is about truly engaging with my heart; it is about being present with what I'm doing.

My whole picture changed once I realized how important it is to be intentional and not just put in the time for the sake of doing so.

This mental and visual exercise helped me figure out a lot of things, many of them in this book, that nudged me to finally take a leap of faith into myself and then pour myself out to others.

Here is how you can do the same exercise: You have a finite amount of unrealized potential in several aspects of life—

emotional and intellectual well-being, relationships, career, wisdom, community, family, athleticism, etc. As life goes on, a bar represents each category within a chart.

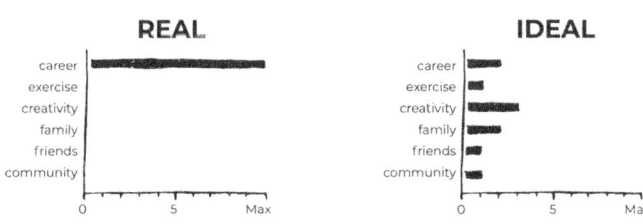

The chart represents the "progress" completed in each category and allows you to discover who you are within each respective field.

After you draw each bar chart with each category of your life, **The Time is Now** to start drawing each bar and its progress: Then, reflect on the size of the bars.

• Career-wise: Is the bar very full?

• Relationships: Am I lacking in this respect?

- Community: Am I engaged with it every now and then?

- Family: Do I only see them on holidays?

- Friends: Do I have a tight circle of friends but see them sporadically?

Now, let's say you can visualize your potential in each area of your life. How would you like the chart to be filled? I invite you to set aside time to reflect and draw in the white box below those areas of most importance in your life presently. Now, be realistic: Do you actually invest your time in these aptitudes or significant matters? Now, be idealistic: How do you want to invest your time? Now, draw a visualization of each chart in this white box.

If you are like me (which you probably are), you may discover that when compared to the reality of your present circumstances, your expectations and aspirations may diverge significantly. That is perfectly normal; we are human beings who sometimes act one way while wishing for something else. The striking concept of visualizing your "potential chart" is that it shows you how much progress you are making in any area of your life and highlights possible improvement areas—if you wish to do so.

Listen, these charts are not meant to categorize you as someone who needs to progress or achieve anything continuously. Rather, the charts are designed to make you reflect on your decisions and the extent to which they align with your true self and how you invest your time.

For me, this exercise showed me how much time I would rather invest in my creative interests, family, my relationships, and my community, and how my actions did not align with these goals—I was focusing more than eighty percent of my time on my career.

Again, if you're like me (which you probably are), you now find the idea of investing most of your time on a career as a complement to your life rather than the central mission of your life.

Through the power of visualization, we can process the striking realities of how we are spending our time as opposed to how we wish to be engaged. And now that we have a better understanding, we can begin to build a path that accommodates our desires.

March Madness: A Month of Relentlessly Pursuing Your Dream

If you have read this book in full, first of all...thank you. You now have made meaningful connections between the ideas it sets forth and circumstances in your personal life and career while reflecting on chimpanzees, fish, Artificial Intelligence, Jim Carrey, and Hip-Hop. Perhaps you have realized how much time you have sacrificed for a future promise that may never materialize; or you have slowly awakened to the fact that the false promise of creative freedom would cost you a forty-year career trajectory, during which you most likely would have been asked to choose between attending family events, spending meaningful time with your friends, exploring your creativity, and moving your career forward.

The paradox of it all is that you have realized that investing forty years while unnecessarily deferring enjoyment until you had free time in the future was a bad deal.

Time is precious. You cannot get it back.

The Book of Genesis begins with the following words: "In the beginning, God spoke the world into existence." This message has stayed with me for my entire life: God knew that the power of the word is unlimited—so unlimited, in fact, it has the potential to create new worlds. Throughout this book, my core intention has been to guide us to a world where our words build new possibilities driven by our authentic selves and refute the false dichotomy telling us that, to be free, we must sacrifice our time for a cause we don't really believe in and our hearts are not aligned to. What really strikes me about the opening sentence of the Book of Genesis is that God's word empowered His actions. That is, if He would not have articulated His words, His vision, and His intentions, actions would not have followed.

It is absolutely true that we cannot build new possibilities with only words, but words are nonetheless essential precursors to making the right decisions as we embark on our creative journey. I hope that my words throughout this book have motivated you to begin putting your new worldview into action—or, I should say, activating the worldview you have already discovered, felt, and nurtured within you.

Working at one of my previous jobs, I used to drive an average of one hour, thirty minutes both ways for a total of three hours' commute each day—for two years. If you do the math, I spent approximately one thousand five hundred sixty hours driving within those two years, which equals sixty-five days wasted in driving. That amounts to 2 months of driving annually. For me, that was way too much time, and I got to a point where it started to make no sense for me to drive that much when I knew I could use that time for something more meaningful (e.g., to write, do interviews, even have a decent breakfast with a friend or a complete workout). I had to leave home way earlier than my peers —and still arrived late—so my morning activities were cut short, and I tried to leave work earlier so my afternoons were not sacrificed too. With all that effort, I would still return home exhausted from working and driving all day, so I had no energy or creative output to focus on myself, my relationships, my friendships, or my creative passions.

On one commute, I called my best friend telling him how it didn't make sense at all, how traffic was, indeed, a dream-killer, and how much more meaningful these three hours could be if I would invest them in something energizing instead of the draining nature of such a long commute.

Then, I had a lightbulb moment: The words I articulated to my friend expanded my worldview. At this stage of my career, I could not add three hours to my day or refuel energy spent on commuting to pursue meaningful activities. However, I could make a promise to myself that whatever time I spent driving (an average of three hours daily), I *had* to invest another three hours devoted to a creative endeavor. In other words, I would compensate for those three "dead hours" by making room for what I loved doing—regardless of time constraints.

With that realization, I sprang into action. I began to see the two-way, three-hour commute as a guidepost for investing in creative activities each day. In doing so, the commute took on a different meaning, and I became excited about long drives.

I began my new game plan at the beginning of March, so I created a "March Madness" challenge with some friends who were experiencing similar frustrations about how they were sacrificing their creative interests for a paycheck, a future, or their work responsibilities. This challenge consisted of committing whatever time any of us wished each day to pursuing our creative interests regardless of their outcome. We would play just for the sake of playing and see where we would end up at the end of the month. To hold each other accountable, we would each record the time spent doing a given activity. The winner would stay honest and keep engaging in the desired activity, and the loser would invite the winner to dinner at a restaurant of the winner's choice.

So, this "March Madness" took on a life of its own: we had a game to play between ourselves, there were stakes, and the price was two-fold—time invested in our creative interests and dinner at our restaurant of choice.

We were energized, pursuing our creativity without an objective in sight. We weren't constrained by metrics other than time spent. So, we didn't evaluate metrics, strive to achieve goals, or set restrictions on ourselves. This was *play* in its purest sense.

The results: My best friend invested an average of fifteen minutes a day to begin writing his novel, describing his experiences as a restauranteur—something he had in the back of his mind for almost his entire career, but he put it on the back burner (no pun intended) for some future date. It became such an energizing activity that he still writes regardless of the time of day.

Another close friend decided she would choose each day to pursue whatever creative feeling she entertained that particular day. So, one day she would write, another she would paint, and others she would brainstorm ideas.

As for me, I decided to invest the time spent on my morning commute engaging in any creative pursuits I had kept dormant. I would split the one hour thirty minutes into three chunks of thirty minutes a day, dedicated to the same activity, to prevent burnout.

During March, I invested forty-five hours into my creative interests, which included writing this book, recording podcast interviews and content for my podcast's social media accounts (which grew one thousand followers and engaged a quarter million people

—which was not my intention at the outset), creating songs, and learning standup comedy, and starting my first company. Even today, I continue all these activities regardless of the outcome. I've even done my very first open-mic standup comedy show and continue to develop my own business, my podcast, and my writing.

The surprises that emerged from these activities have truly caught me off guard—so much so, the energy I felt during just that one March gave me enough confidence to walk my talk and take a Sabbatical to explore my creativity full-time.

When March Madness began, I had no intention whatsoever of quitting my job, no intention of growing my podcast following, and no intention of deciding to focus full-time on this book. Instead, I was simply interested in finally giving myself time to allow my creativity to emerge and see where life leads me.

The purpose of this challenge is not to encourage you to take any risks you are uncomfortable with or cannot realistically afford. It is an invitation to put your words into action; it is an opportunity to create your world through your word; it is also a great way of tapping into your creative inclinations and shaping them in concrete terms—and setting rules—yet at the same time giving space for the creative nuances to emerge freely and allowing yourself to be surprised at the end of the month by how much you have accomplished without having an objective in the first place (it doesn't have to be in March, by the way).

This challenge is our way of building a world where we put our creativity first and allow it to guide us to what truly gives us energy and life. It's a statement we declare to ourselves, affirming that we will not wait any longer to pursue what makes us human, what makes us alive, what makes us powerful creative forces of nature.

It is our way of saying: The Time is Now To Honor Our Time On Earth, committing ourselves to realizing our creative potential, today!

Pause and Ponder: Chapter Thirteen

• Do you want to sacrifice overall happiness to increase your net worth? (Are these mutually exclusive?)

• Do you really want to track every aspect of our lives to optimize your time on Earth, improving irrelevant, abstract metrics while looking the other way and failing to face your challenges?

• Do you really want to take orders all your life from lost people who caught themselves inside the Matrix and now want to entrap you, too?

• Do you really want to sacrifice the prime of your life to save enough money for retirement instead of enjoying the things that already make you happy?

• Go back to the "Thinking About Our Life In Charts" Subchapter and review your life charts. Allow your feelings and thoughts to emerge with no intervention.

• Go back to the "March Madness" Subchapter and try to build your own challenge with your friends; add stakes, make it friendly, and make it challenging—Go play!

• **Are You Ready To Honor Your Time On Earth?**

NOTES

Introduction

1. https://www.investopedia.com/millennial-homeownership-still-lagging-behind-previous-generations-7510642#:~:text=Key%20Take-aways,were%20at%20the%20same%20age

1. The Hardest Battle You Will Ever Face

1. Schroeder, Jules. "Millennials, This Is What Your Quarter-Life Crisis Is Telling You." Forbes. September 8, 2016. https://www.forbes.com/sites/julesschroeder/2016/09/08/millennials-this-is-what-your-quarter-life-crisis-is-telling-you/?sh=440c1d273262.
2. 2. Harriet Johnston "The celebrity 'monk' who married Bennifer: How London-born Jay Shetty went from troubled schoolboy to a career in finance before leaving for an Indian Ashram - then became a motivational speaker and friend to the stars." *Daily Mail*, August 22, 2022. https://www.dailymail.co.uk/femail/article-11133681/Monk-Jay-Shetty-went-experimenting-drinks-drugs-London-marrying-J-Lo.html.
3. 3. Shetty, Jay. *Think like a monk: Train your mind for peace and purpose every day*. Simon and Schuster, 2020.
4. The Zebra. "Housing Trends Visualized." Accessed June 22, 2024. https://www.thezebra.com/resources/home/housing-trends-visualized/#:~:text=Using%20data%20from%20the%20U.S.,to%2Dincome%20ratio%20of%202.1.
5. U.S. Census Bureau. "Income and Poverty in the United States: 2021." *U.S. Census Bureau*, September 2022. https://www.census.gov/library/publications/2022/demo/p60-276.html.
6. "Baby Boomers." *Britannica*. Accessed May 14, 2024. https://www.britannica.com/topic/baby-boomers.
7. Economic Policy Institute. "The Productivity–Pay Gap." Accessed June 22, 2024. https://www.epi.org/productivity-pay-gap/#:~:text=From%201979%20to%202020%2C%20net,(after%20adjusting%20for%20inflation).
8. Economic Policy Institute. "The Productivity–Pay Gap." Accessed June 22, 2024. https://www.epi.org/productivity-pay-gap/#:~:text=From%201979%20to%202020%2C%20net,(after%20adjusting%20for%20inflation).
9. Nova, Annie. "58% of Americans Are Living Paycheck to Paycheck, CNBC Survey Reveals." *CNBC*, April 11, 2023. https://www.cnbc.com/2023/04/11/58percent-of-americans-are-living-paycheck-to-paycheck-cnbc-survey-reveals.html.

10. Nuckols, William, Kim E. Bullington, and Dennis E. Gregory. "Was it worth it? Using student loans to finance a college degree." *Higher Education Politics & Economics* 6.1 (2020): 1-19.
11. Taleb, Nassim Nicholas. *The bed of Procrustes: Philosophical and practical aphorisms*. Vol. 4. Random House, 2010.
12. Skinner, Burrhus F. "Reinforcement today." *American Psychologist* 13.3 (1958): 94.

2. Our Time Will Time Us

1. GHE: Life expectancy and healthy life expectancy https://www.who.int/data/gho/data/themes/mortality-and-global-health-estimates/ghe-life-expectancy-and-healthy-life-expectancy
2. Through Conversations Podcast Interview Kyle Kowalski - https://www.youtube.com/watch?v=jfgFBLLsWtc
3. Through Conversations Podcast Interview With Kieran Setiya - https://www.youtube.com/watch?v=qqjDdb2i5Kk
4. Burnout as a Cause for Job Dissatisfaction https://www.phoenix.edu/content/dam/edu/career-institute/doc/burnout-banton-garza.pdf
5. Post on X - https://x.com/NavalismHQ/status/1419107633391411200
6. Paul Tien-Lin Ho Ephrem, "Retirement and Life Span," Faculty of Engineering, King Fahd University of Petroleum & Minerals, 1999, https://faculty.kfupm.edu.sa/COE/gutub/English_Misc/Retire1.htm.
7. Hugo Westerlund, et al., "Effect of retirement on major chronic conditions and fatigue: French GAZEL occupational cohort study," *BMJ (Clinical research ed.)* vol. 341, Nov. 23, 2010, doi:10.1136/bmj.c6149, https://pubmed.ncbi.nlm.nih.gov/21098617/.
8. Kachan, D., Fleming, L. E., Christ, S., Muennig, P., Prado, G., Tannenbaum, S. L., et. al. (n.d.). "Health Status of Older U.S. Workers and Nonworkers, National Health Interview Survey, 1997-2011." November 10, 2023. [URL: https://pubmed.ncbi.nlm.nih.gov/21098617/].
9. Harvard Health. *Harvard Health Publishing*, 2022. "Working Later in Life Can Pay Off in More Than Just Income." https://www.health.harvard.edu/staying-healthy/working-later-in-life-can-pay-off-in-more-than-just-income.
10. Südhof, Thomas C., and Robert C. Malenka. "Understanding synapses: past, present, and future." *Neuron* 60, no. 3 (2008): 469-476.

3. The Layered Later

1. Sam Altman Interview - https://www.youtube.com/watch?v=uEl2KUZ3JWA&t=1580s
2. Paul Portesi on X - https://x.com/PaulPortesi/status/1553966469733527557
3. Tilo, Dexter. "77% of Employees Would Sacrifice Their Personal Life for Career Success." Human Resources Director, 23 Jun 2022, https://www.

hcamag.com/ca/specialization/employment-law/77-of-employees-would-sacrifice-their-personal-life-for-career-success/410697.
4. Financial Post. "In choosing a job, people focus on the money but forget about the important stuff." The New York Times, 9 March 2017, https://financialpost.com/executive/careers/in-choosing-a-job-people-focus-on-the-money-but-forget-about-the-important-stuff.
5. "Ten Million or One More Day to Live." The Networker. https://www.youtube.com/watch?v=sesbol90R9M
6. Through Conversations Podcast Interview With Chris Williamson - https://www.youtube.com/watch?v=MTMuihAoHjU
7. Chris Williamson on X - https://twitter.com/ChrisWillx/status/1599841032115433472
8. Dass, Ram. *Be Here Now.* United States, Harmony/Rodale, 2010.

4. Bio-Wired to Hunt Success

1. The Psychology (and Biology) of Love - https://www.denverpsychotherapygroup.com/blog/the-psychology-and-biology-of-love
2. People with an evolutionarily-mismatched lifestyle are more likely to face several negative outcomes - https://www.psypost.org/people-with-an-evolutionary-mismatched-lifestyle-are-more-likely-to-face-several-negative-outcomes/?utm_source=chatgpt.com#google_vignette
   Melissa B Manus, Evolutionary mismatch, Evolution, Medicine, and Public Health, Volume 2018, Issue 1, 2018, Pages 190–191, https://doi.org/10.1093/emph/eoy023
3. Morris, Chris. "Gen Z, Millennial Workers Stressed Out: Alight Research." Fortune, October 4, 2023. https://fortune.com/2023/10/04/gen-z-millennial-workers-stressed-out-alight-research/.
4. Through Conversations Podcast Interview With Dr. Da Silva - https://www.youtube.com/watch?v=NaiWZvFe6Kg
5. Merzenich, Hiltrud, Hajo Zeeb, and Maria Blettner. "Decreasing sperm quality: a global problem?." BMC public health 10.1 (2010): 1-5.
6. Evans-Hoeker, Emily A et al. "Major depression, antidepressant use, and male and female fertility." Fertility and sterility vol. 109,5 (2018): 879-887. doi:10.1016/j.fertnstert.2018.01.029
7. Lapane, K L et al. "Is a history of depressive symptoms associated with an increased risk of infertility in women?." Psychosomatic medicine vol. 57,6 (1995): 509-13; discussion 514-6. doi:10.1097/00006842-199511000-00001
8. CDC. "Infertility and Impaired Fecundity in the United States, 1982–2010: Data From the National Survey of Family Growth." Hyattsville, MD: National Center for Health Statistics, 2012. Web. 7 Aug. 2023. https://www.cdc.gov/nchs/data/nhsr/nhsr067.pdf. CDC. "Births: Provisional Data for 2018." Hyattsville, MD: National Center for Health Statistics, 2018. Web. 7 Aug. 2023. https://www.cdc.gov/nchs/data/vsrr/vsrr-007-508.pdf.
9. The Psychology (and Biology) of Love - https://www.denverpsychotherapygroup.com/blog/the-psychology-and-biology-of-love

10. Storr, Will. (2021) 2021. *The Status Game*. [Edition unavailable]. Harper-Collins Publishers. https://www.perlego.com/book/1982067/the-status-game-how-social-position-governs-everything-pdf.

11. Through Conversations Podcast Interview With Will Storr - https://www.youtube.com/watch?v=YQzr-3PtqbM

12. Through Conversations Podcast Interview With David Buss - https://www.youtube.com/watch?v=c9FXnA9jRdg

13. Anderson, C., Hildreth, J. A. D., & Howland, L. (2015). Is the desire for status a fundamental human motive? A review of the empirical literature. *Psychological bulletin*, *141*(3), 574–601. https://doi.org/10.1037/a0038781

14. Evolutionary Psychology, David Buss (Routledge, 2015), p. 11.

15. 21 Savage Song - https://genius.com/21-savage-and-metro-boomin-rich-nigga-shit-lyrics

16. Successful, by Drake- https://genius.com/Drake-successful-lyrics

17. von Rueden, Christopher et al. "Why do men seek status? Fitness payoffs to dominance and prestige." Proceedings. Biological sciences vol. 278,1715 (2011): 2223-32. doi:10.1098/rspb.2010.2145.

18. von Rueden, Christopher et al. "Why do men seek status? Fitness payoffs to dominance and prestige." Proceedings. Biological sciences vol. 278,1715 (2011): 2223-32. doi:10.1098/rspb.2010.2145.

19. Irons, W. (1979). Cultural and biological success. *Evolutionary biology and human social behavior: An anthropological perspective*, *284*, 302.

20. Miller, Geoffrey. *The Mating Mind: How Sexual Choice Shaped the Evolution of Human Nature*. Anchor, 2011.

21. Veblen, Thorstein. *Conspicuous consumption*. Vol. 38. Penguin UK, 2005. pp. 210-211

22. Miller, Geoffrey. *The Mating Mind: How Sexual Choice Shaped the Evolution of Human Nature*. Anchor, 2011.

23. Garcia, Kate Payne. "UM Cost of Attendance Will Rise Slightly in 2024-2025." *WLRN*, April 8, 2024. https://www.wlrn.org/education/2024-04-08/um-university-miami-cost-attendance-2024-2025.

24. Beal, Mary, Mary O. Borg, and Harriet A. Stranahan. "The onus of student debt: Who is most impacted by the rising cost of higher education?." International Research Journal of Applied Finance 10.8 (2019): 219-231.

25. Demos. 'The Leg Up: How a Privileged Minority Is Graduating Without Debt.' Accessed October 5, 2023. https://www.demos.org/research/leg-how-privileged-minority-graduating-without-debt.

26. College Board. 'Who Borrows Most? Bachelor's Degree Recipients with High Levels of Student Loan Debt.' 2010. https://research.collegeboard.org/media/pdf/trends-2010-who-borrows-most-brief.pdf.

27. Guan, N., Guariglia, A., Moore, P., Xu, F., & Al-Janabi, H. (2022). Financial stress and depression in adults: A systematic review. *PloS one*, *17*(2), e0264041. https://doi.org/10.1371/journal.pone.0264041

28. Branden, Nathaniel. *Six Pillars of Self-Esteem: The Definitive Work on Self-Esteem by the Leading Pioneer in the Field*. Bantam, 1995.

29. Storr, Will. The Status Game: On Human Life and How to Play It (p. 39). HarperCollins Publishers. Kindle Edition.

30. Ok, E., Qian, Y., Strejcek, B., & Aquino, K. (2020, July 2). Signaling Virtuous Victimhood as Indicators of Dark Triad Personalities. Journal of Personality and Social Psychology. Advance online publication. http://dx.doi.org/10.1037/pspp0000329

31. Buss, David M. "The science of human mating strategies: An historical perspective." *Psychological Inquiry* 24.3 (2013): 171-177.

32. Social Media Dopamine: The Hidden Addiction Behind Your Screen Time https://neurolaunch.com/social-media-dopamine/?utm_source=chatgpt.com

33. Naval Ravikant post on X- https://x.com/NavalismHQ/status/1613604472667635729?lang=es

34. Through Conversations Podcast: Full episode with Anna Lembke - https://www.youtube.com/watch?v=WKngZF0e8O4

35. Lembke, Anna. Dopamine nation: Finding balance in the age of indulgence. Penguin, 2021.

5. The Alchemy of Gut Feelings

1. Klein, Gary. The power of intuition: How to use your gut feelings to make better decisions at work. Currency, 2004.

2. Conor, Steve. "Psychologist Gary Klein has helped the US President make critical decisions and analysed the 'pathways' to Eureka moments." Independent, 9 April 2015, https://www.independent.co.uk/life-style/health-and-families/features/psychologist-gary-klein-has-helped-the-us-president-make-critical-decisions-and-analysed-the-pathways-to-eureka-moments-10163583.html.

3. Klein, Gary. "Expert intuition and naturalistic decision making." Handbook of intuition research (2011): 69-78.

4. Oktar, Kerem, and Tania Lombrozo. "Deciding to be authentic: Intuition is favored over deliberation when authenticity matters." Cognition 223 (2022): 105021.

5. Kandasamy, N., Garfinkel, S., Page, L. et al. Interoceptive Ability Predicts Survival on a London Trading Floor. Sci Rep 6, 32986 (2016). https://doi.org/10.1038/srep32986

6. Through Conversations Podcast: Full Episode With Annie Murphy Paul - https://www.youtube.com/watch?v=arDIvtCEKmk

7. Paul, Annie Murphy. *The Extended Mind: The Power of Thinking Outside the Brain*. Eamon Dolan Books, 2021.

8. Kandasamy, N., Garfinkel, S., Page, L. et al. Interoceptive Ability Predicts Survival on a London Trading Floor. Sci Rep 6, 32986 (2016). https://doi.org/10.1038/srep32986

9. Blakeslee, Sandra. "In Work on Intuition, Gut Feelings Are Tracked to Source in the Brain." *The New York Times*, March 4, 1997. https://www.nytimes.com/1997/03/04/science/in-work-on-intuition-gut-feelings-are-tracked-to-source-the-brain.html.

10. Paul, Annie Murphy. *The Extended Mind: The Power of Thinking Outside the Brain*. Eamon Dolan Books, 2021.
11. Paul, Annie Murphy. *The Extended Mind: The Power of Thinking Outside the Brain*. Eamon Dolan Books, 2021.
12. Marcuse, Herbert. One-dimensional man: Studies in the ideology of advanced industrial society. Routledge, 2013.
13. Marcuse, Herbert. One-dimensional man: Studies in the ideology of advanced industrial society. Routledge, 2013.

6. Stop Polishing a False Diamond

1. The Decline of Neuroplasticity: Why Learning Becomes Harder as We Age." *Mind Memory Research*. Accessed July 17, 2024. https://mindmemoryre search.com/cognitive-decline/the-decline-of-neuroplasticity-why-learning-becomes-harder-as-we-age
2. Haita-Falah, Corina. "Sunk-cost fallacy and cognitive ability in individual decision-making." *Journal of Economic Psychology* 58 (2017): 44-59.
3. Through Conversations Podcast Interview With Chris Williamson - https://www.youtube.com/watch?v=MTMuihAoHjU
4. Marcus, Aubrey. "Chris Williamson: The Codes To A Life of Happiness and Meaning" YouTube, uploaded by Aubrey Marcus, June 29, 2022. https://www.youtube.com/watch?v=yX4XP6Pes5E.

7. Slay The Serpent

1. Anu Atluru post - https://twitter.com/anuatluru/status/1802812023467594121
2. Dawkins, Richard. "The Selfish Meme." *Time* 153.15 (1999): 52-53.
3. Jaffe, Aniela. "Memories, dreams, reflections by CG Jung." *Trans. Richard and Clara* (1961).
4. Blue Cross Blue Shield. "Major Depression: The Impact on Overall Health." The Health of America Report. Accessed May 14, 2024. https://www.bcbs.com/the-health-of-america/reports.
5. Oaklander, Mandy. "Major Depression Diagnosis Is on the Rise." Time, May 10, 2018. https://time.com/5271244/major-depression-diagnosis-spike/.
6. Oaklander, Mandy. "Major Depression Diagnosis Is on the Rise." Time, May 10, 2018. https://time.com/5271244/major-depression-diagnosis-spike/.

8. Integrating Life and Work

1. Vervaeke, John, Christopher Mastropietro, and Filip Miscevic. *Zombies in Western culture: a twenty-first century crisis*. Open Book Publishers, 2017.
2. Gurdjieff, George. *The herald of coming good*. Book Studio, 2008.
3. *Fortune*. 2022. "The Soft Life of DAR." September 11. https://fortune.com/2022/09/11/the-soft-life-of-dar/

4. *Steve Jobs Archive.* "Put Something Back." Accessed June 22, 2024. https://putsomethingback.stevejobsarchive.com/
5. Through Conversations, Full episode with Nicholas Christakis - https://www.youtube.com/watch?v=fCdRMzejLJ0&t=2297s
6. Christakis, Nicholas A. Blueprint: The evolutionary origins of a good society. Hachette UK, 2019.
7. Christakis, Nicholas A. Blueprint: The evolutionary origins of a good society. Hachette UK, 2019.
8. Christakis, Nicholas A. Blueprint: The evolutionary origins of a good society. Hachette UK, 2019.
9. *Trustbridge Global.* 2021. "Giving Science Proves It's Good for Your Health: 3 Physical and Mental Benefits of Giving." March 25. Accessed June 22, 2024. https://www.trustbridgeglobal.com/blog/2021/3/25/giving-science-proves-its-good-for-your-health-3-physical-and-mental-benefits-of-giving
10. Dossey, Larry. "The Helper's High." Explore (New York, N.Y.) vol. 14,6 (2018): 393-399. doi:10.1016/j.explore.2018.10.003
11. Christakis, Nicholas A. Blueprint: The evolutionary origins of a good society. Hachette UK, 2019.
12. *Fortune.* 2022. "The Soft Life of DAR." September 11. https://fortune.com/2022/09/11/the-soft-life-of-dar/
13. *Fortune.* 2022. "The Soft Life of DAR." September 11. https://fortune.com/2022/09/11/the-soft-life-of-dar/
14. *Fortune.* 2022. "The Soft Life of DAR." September 11. https://fortune.com/2022/09/11/the-soft-life-of-dar/
15. Neil deGrasse Tyson Tells His Life Story (Full Interview) by djvlad - https://www.youtube.com/watch?v=vXmGPALbTKA&t=2096s
16. Neil deGrasse Tyson Tells His Life Story (Full Interview) by djvlad - https://www.youtube.com/watch?v=vXmGPALbTKA&t=2096s
17. Neil deGrasse Tyson Tells His Life Story (Full Interview) by djvlad - https://www.youtube.com/watch?v=vXmGPALbTKA&t=2096s
18. Tyson, Neil deGrasse. *Starry Messenger: Cosmic perspectives on civilization.* Henry Holt and Company, 2022.
19. Yaden, David B., et al. "The overview effect: Awe and self-transcendent experience in space flight." Psychology of Consciousness: Theory, Research, and Practice 3.1 (2016): 1.
20. Yaden, David B., et al. "The overview effect: Awe and self-transcendent experience in space flight." Psychology of Consciousness: Theory, Research, and Practice 3.1 (2016): 1.
21. Tyson, Neil deGrasse. *Starry Messenger: Cosmic perspectives on civilization.* Henry Holt and Company, 2022.
22. Tyson, Neil deGrasse. *Starry Messenger: Cosmic perspectives on civilization.* Henry Holt and Company, 2022.

9. The Art of Catching Serendipity

1. Hopkins, Jerry. *Elvis: the biography*. Plexus Publishing, 2014.
2. Stanley, Kenneth O., and Joel Lehman. *Why greatness cannot be planned: The myth of the objective*. Springer, 2015.
3. Stanley, Kenneth O., and Joel Lehman. *Why greatness cannot be planned: The myth of the objective*. Springer, 2015.
4. Stanley, Kenneth O., and Joel Lehman. *Why greatness cannot be planned: The myth of the objective*. Springer, 2015.
5. MacMullan, Jackie, Rafe Bartholomew, and Dan Klores. *Basketball: A Love Story*. Crown, 2019.
6. Stanley, Kenneth O., and Joel Lehman. *Why greatness cannot be planned: The myth of the objective*. Springer, 2015.
7. Stanley, Kenneth O., and Joel Lehman. *Why greatness cannot be planned: The myth of the objective*. Springer, 2015.
8. Stanley, Kenneth O., and Joel Lehman. *Why greatness cannot be planned: The myth of the objective*. Springer, 2015.
9. Stanley, Kenneth O., and Joel Lehman. *Why greatness cannot be planned: The myth of the objective*. Springer, 2015.
10. Stanley, Kenneth O., and Joel Lehman. *Why greatness cannot be planned: The myth of the objective*. Springer, 2015.
11. Stanley, Kenneth O., and Joel Lehman. *Why greatness cannot be planned: The myth of the objective*. Springer, 2015.
12. Experimental Learning - Why Greatness Cannot Be Planned: A Summary https://www.youtube.com/watch?v=9Uc2Rvhn1wc
13. Nova, Annie. "Job Unhappiness Is at a Staggering All-Time High, According to Gallup." *CNBC*, August 12, 2022. https://www.cnbc.com/2022/08/12/job-unhappiness-is-at-a-staggering-all-time-high-according-to-gallup.html.
14. Jim Carrey at MIU: Commencement Address at the 2014 Graduation, available at https://youtu.be/V80-gPkpH6M
15. Jim Carrey at MIU: Commencement Address at the 2014 Graduation, available at https://youtu.be/V80-gPkpH6M
16. Jim Carrey at MIU: Commencement Address at the 2014 Graduation, available at https://youtu.be/V80-gPkpH6M
17. Jim Carrey at MIU: Commencement Address at the 2014 Graduation, available at https://youtu.be/V80-gPkpH6M

10. The Freedom of Risk

1. Founders Podcast post on X https://x.com/FoundersPodcast/status/1698359650129711563
2. Kendrick Lamar, Mirror lyrics - https://genius.com/Kendrick-lamar-mirror-lyrics
3. Cott, Brittany. "Do Identical Twins Have the Same Fingerprints?" *Healthline*. Accessed June 22, 2024. https://www.healthline.com/health/do-identical-twins-have-the-same-

fingerprints#:~:text=But%2C%20-
like%20those%20who%20aren,have%20the%20exact%20same%20fin-
gerprints.

11. How We All Can Navigate the Gen Z Economy

1. **Pooley, Gale.** "We're All Billionaires Now." *Substack*. Accessed December 17, 2024. https://galepooley.substack.com/p/were-all-billionaires-now.
2. Joe Rogan Experience #1309 - Naval Ravikant - https://www.youtube.com/watch?v=3qHkcs3kG44
3. Mollman, Steve 'CEO is so worried about remote workers using A.I. and doing multiple jobs he threatens to increase quotas by '30 to 50 times our normal production' *Yahoo Finance*, April 21, 2023. https://finance.yahoo.com/news/ceo-worried-remote-workers-using-174658960.html.
4. Through Conversations Podcast - Jim O'Shaughnessy - The Tao of Jim, The Matrix, and The Stock Market - https://www.youtube.com/watch?v=Nvjf5i I_gPM
5. Post by James O'Shaughnessy on X https://twitter.com/jposhaughnessy/status/1655237860981628928
6. Ford, Brody. "IBM to pause hiring for 'Back-office'jobs that AI could kill." *Bloomberg, may* (2023).
7. Through Conversations Podcast Interview With Neil deGrasse Tyson - https://www.youtube.com/watch?v=08Of8uTAZBo&t=2s
8. Through Conversations Podcast Interview With Neil deGrasse Tyson - https://www.youtube.com/watch?v=08Of8uTAZBo&t=2s
9. Through Conversations Podcast Interview With Neil deGrasse Tyson - https://www.youtube.com/watch?v=08Of8uTAZBo&t=2s
10. "The Curious Beginnings of Morning Brew." *Medium*. Accessed December 17, 2024. https://medium.com/small-mighty/the-curious-beginnings-of-morning-brew-44924158049.
11. "The Skimm: Danielle Weisberg & Carly Zakin." *Into The Gloss*. Published January 2015. https://intothegloss.com/2015/01/the-skimm-danielle-weisberg-carly-zakin/.
12. xAI website - https://x.ai
13. Navalism on X - https://x.com/NavalismHQ/status/1774726647557571012
14. Tesla CEO Elon Musk: I'll say what I want to say, and if we lose money, so be it -https://www.youtube.com/watch?v=6sUwRiIncKU
15. Taleb, Nassim Nicholas. The black swan: The impact of the highly improbable. Vol. 2. Random house, 2007. Page 208.
16. Post by Naval Ravikant on X - https://twitter.com/naval/status/1054984950192181248?lang=en
17. Taleb, Nassim Nicholas. The black swan: The impact of the highly improbable. Vol. 2. Random house, 2007.
18. Watts, Duncan, and Gardiner Morse. "The science behind six degrees." *Harvard business review* 81.2 (2003): 16-17.

19. Watts, Duncan J., and Steven H. Strogatz. "Collective dynamics of 'small-world' networks." nature 393.6684 (1998): 440-442.
20. Smith, David. "Proof! Just six degrees of separation between us." *The Guardian* 2 (2008).
21. Taleb, Nassim Nicholas. *Fooled by randomness: The hidden role of chance in life and in the markets*. Editeurs divers USA, 2016.
    BEN CASNOCHA - https://casnocha.com/2008/06/nassim-talebs-t.html
22. BEN CASNOCHA - https://casnocha.com/2008/06/nassim-talebs-t.html
23. Through Conversations Podcast - Victor Levy: The Most Important Truths You Need to Know to Live a Fulfilling Life - https://www.youtube.com/watch?v=tY2I6h8X4bo
24. Levy, Victor. *Life Is Setting Me up for Success*. Balboa Press, 2021.

12. Build Your Own Paris

1. Mendes, Sam. 2008. Revolutionary Road. United States: DreamWorks Distribution.
2. How Amanda Hesser Cooked up Success." *Venture Voice* (Substack). Accessed December 17, 2024. https://venturevoice.substack.com/p/how-amanda-hesser-cooked-up-success.
3. Goldberg, Daniel, and Linus Larsson. Minecraft: The real inside story of Markus' Notch'Persson and the gaming phenomenon of the century. Virgin Books, 2015.
4. **Ferriss, Tim.** "Fear-Setting: The Most Valuable Exercise I Do Every Month." *The Blog of Author Tim Ferriss*. Published May 15, 2017. https://tim.blog/2017/05/15/fear-setting/.
5. Navalism post on X - https://x.com/NavalismHQ/status/1860172421699109343

13. The Life Principles of Via Negativa

1. Taleb, Nassim Nicholas. *Skin in the game: Hidden asymmetries in daily life*. Random House, 2018.
2. Wilson, Nigel. "Millennials And Housing, Part 3: How Wage Stagnation Has Flipped The Housing Equation." *Forbes*, December 18, 2021. https://www.forbes.com/sites/nigelwilson/2021/12/18/millennials-and-housing-part-3-how-wage-stagnation-has-flipped-the-housing-equation/.
3. Alex Levy Post on X - https://x.com/alex_levox/status/1732215344419176795
4. "A Virtual Life." *Insight: The Chicago School Magazine*. Accessed December 17, 2024. https://www.thechicagoschool.edu/insight/from-the-magazine/a-virtual-life/.

ACKNOWLEDGMENTS

It's surreal to think that this book is finished. The journey of writing it has been one of the most profound experiences of my life. Every conversation I've had—whether with a stranger at the gym, a friend over coffee, or a guest on my podcast—has shaped the ideas in these pages. Hearing others reflect on how they can honor their time on Earth, tap into their creative potential, redefine their relationship with work and purpose, and explore the possibilities of life in the age of AI has been inspiring beyond measure.

Writing this book has replenished my life energy, and it's my sincerest wish that at least one idea within these pages sparks something in you—something that ignites the fire you know is already in your heart.

And so, first and foremost, I want to thank you, the reader. It might be unconventional to say this here, but your time and attention mean the world to me, and I'm grateful for your willingness to explore these ideas with me—if you enjoyed this book, consider sharing it with a loved one and leaving a review.

To my incredible editors—Gabriella Gafni, Rachael S., and Jaime Brockway—thank you for your insights, guidance, and genuine enthusiasm for this project. Working with you has been an absolute joy.

To Daniel Morgenstern, who created the stunning illustrations for this book—you are a creative genius, and your work brought this project to life in ways I couldn't have imagined.

To James Jones, who went above and beyond in designing the cover—you captured the essence of this book perfectly, and I am forever grateful.

To my friends and family—thank you for always supporting my crazy ideas. Your belief in me has carried me through every step of this journey.

With love,

Alex

ABOUT THE AUTHOR

Alex Levy is a former speechwriter and creator of ThroughConversations.com, a podcast with over 75,000 subscribers (at the time of writing) and more than 25 million views that explores the truth through conversations with the most brilliant minds, exploring topics at the intersection of creativity, technology, and personal growth. With experience at xAI, Alex is well-versed in the challenges and opportunities of the modern workplace with the rise of technological innovations. He has been recognized for his ability to engage with leading thinkers like Noam Chomsky, Neil deGrasse Tyson, and Kevin Kelly, bringing fresh perspectives to a global audience. Beyond his professional pursuits, Alex enjoys doing standup comedy, which adds a unique flavor to his storytelling. He splits his time between Miami and Mexico City.

Visit timeisnowbook.com to learn more.

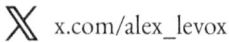 x.com/alex_levox

Printed in Dunstable, United Kingdom